A CAVALCADE OF
SEA LEGENDS

From many a wondrous grot and secret cell
Unnumber'd and enormous polypi
Winnow with giant arms the slumbering green.

Tennyson—*The Kraken*

A CAVALCADE OF

SEA LEGENDS

EDITED BY
MICHAEL BROWN

ILLUSTRATED BY
KRYSTYNA TURSKA

NEW YORK
HENRY Z. WALCK, INC.

First published in Great Britain 1971
as The Hamish Hamilton Book of Sea Legends
© 1971 MICHAEL BROWN
Illustrations © 1971 KRYSTYNA TURSKA
All rights reserved
ISBN: 0–8098–2419–1
Library of Congress Catalog Card Number: 77–175941

Printed in Great Britain

Contents

Introduction

THE sea is the last of the world's great mysteries. Man has explored the continents, climbed the highest mountains, traversed the Poles, sent men to the moon, but the depths of the ocean are still uncharted. More than two-thirds of our globe is covered by sea and yet our knowledge of what lies beneath the surface is limited to a depth of no more than six hundred feet, the maximum depth that a free diver wearing aqualung equipment has reached. It is true that Professor Picard achieved a depth of 6·78 miles in his bathyscaphe, but a pressure chamber like this can only take up a fixed position on the sea-bed and is restricted by its life lines to the ship above so that exploration is confined to the immediate surroundings only.

It is hardly surprising then that mankind should have invented a great many myths and legends in an effort to interpret an element so hostile, so strange and so secret. For not only has the kingdom under the waves remained impenetrable (the deepest an unaided swimmer has ever managed is 120 feet) but the surface itself can change so rapidly and radically, according to the weather conditions, that to an unscientific mind it would seem as if the sea were ruled by the most capricious of Gods.

And yet the sea is also a rich source of food and has often served as a powerful protector to maritime peoples who have learned the arts of seamanship, so that a small power like the Greeks could defeat a large land-based power like the Persians because of their superior sea-skill. Again, in the days when journeys on land were extremely dangerous because of brigandage and inadequate protection for travellers the sea often provided the safest trade routes. It also produced peoples like the Vikings or Polynesians so completely adapted to a seafaring life that they were able to sail for thousands of miles in their small boats, looking for new lands to settle.

So, man's feeling for the sea has always been ambivalent—a love-hate relationship. It is well summed up in the words of a Scottish fisherman: "She is like a woman whose beauty is dreadful and who breaks your heart at last whether she smiles or frowns. But she doesn't care about that, or whether you are hurt or not. It is because she has no heart, being all wild water." The gods of the sea are unpredictable beings who are to be feared, propitiated, served, but at all costs never offended.

The idea behind this anthology has been to illustrate the kinds of legends and folk-lore that naturally evolve when people whose daily lives are closely bound up with the sea find themselves faced by strange phenomena for which they have no rational explanation. As might be expected such legends tend to have much in common no matter what their country of origin. Stories of mermaids and mermen, for example, are to be found in countries with rocky coastlines all over the world.

The greater part of the material in this book is drawn from Classical, Teutonic and Celtic Sources. This is only natural because these three strands make up a fine tradition of European folk-lore that is much more readily accessible than, say, the legends of China and Japan, however good the latter may be.

Inevitably some of the stories I have chosen will be familiar; The "Flying Dutchman" is an obvious example. But some are relatively unknown, although still, I think, extremely interesting. I find Jonas Lie's tales, in particular, with their strange blend of harsh realism and supernatural horrors, have a peculiar fascination which I hope others will share.

The division of the book into three sections seemed a natural one when I started collecting material, but I am aware that the last part is perhaps less strong than the other two. Mythical voyages of the kind represented are not as numerous as one might think and to find stories entirely restricted to adventures at sea is impossible. At some point the ship must touch land and if the hero spends too much time there I can only crave the reader's indulgence and remind him that even the most indefatigable sailor must have some shore leave if the voyage is not to grow stale.

M.B.

I

Mermaids and Monsters

The Mermaid

ANON

Of all the legendary inhabitants of the sea Mermaids are the best known and loved. Nowadays they are always shown with a fish's tail, a tradition which goes back at least as far as the Romans. But this was not always the case; sometimes the tail was forked, ending in two fins (this is often to be seen in Romanesque sculpture), whilst in many stories the Mermaid is no more than a young woman whose natural element is the sea.

Most Mermaids are harmless creatures easily swept off their tails by the charms of handsome young fishermen with whom they often live for many years before, without warning, they are called back to their home beneath the waves.

There are, however, some mermaids the sight of whom bodes no good for the mariner. They are descended from the sirens whose sweet singing lured brave sailors to destruction. In the following ballad the meeting with the mermaid is a bad omen, although the captain has already courted disaster by daring to set sail on a Friday.

One Friday morn when we set sail,
   Not very far from land,
We there did espy a fair pretty maid
    With a comb and a glass in her hand, her hand, her
      hand,
    With a comb and a glass in her hand.
      While the raging seas did roar,
        And the stormy winds did blow,
      While we jolly sailor-boys were up into the top
        And the land-lubbers lying down below, below
        below,
        And the land-lubbers lying down below.

Then up starts the captain of our gallant ship,
    And a brave young man was he:
"I've a wife and child in fair Bristol town,
    But a widow I fear she will be."

Then up starts the mate of our gallant ship,
    And a bold young man was he:
"Oh! I have a wife in fair Portsmouth town,
    But a widow I fear she will be."

Then up starts the cook of our gallant ship,
    And a gruff old soul was he:
"Oh! I have a wife in fair Plymouth town,
    But a widow I fear she will be."

And then up spoke the little cabin-boy,
    And a pretty little boy was he;
"Oh! I am more grievd for my daddy and my mammy
    Than you for your wives all three."

Then three times round went our gallant ship,
    And three times round went she;
For the want of a life-boat they all went down,
    And she sank to the bottom of the sea.

The Mermaid of Emmeloord

JAN DE HARTOG

THIS is the story of a girl called Mensje who lived in Emmeloord, a windswept village of small red houses huddled close together, on the Island of Schokland peeping over the dike at the Zuider Zee.

Mensje had a lover called Jan Viool who was a sailor for the East India Company. They were to marry after his next voyage, and Mensje had started fitting out her hope chest when one night she had a curious dream.

She saw Jan standing at the bottom of a broken red tower. She couldn't make out whether it was night or day for the light was very strange: a curious blue that sometimes changed to green. The tower was covered with a sort of creeper the like of which she had never seen before. Jan stood there, clad only in his trousers, a blood-soaked kerchief knotted around his head, and he was calling her. The curious thing was that although she saw him calling she didn't hear a sound. She saw his mouth move in a deep heavy silence, as if he was trying to make himself heard through a thick glass plate. She tried to understand what he was calling and he tried to make himself understood, but the heavy silence was impenetrable, and she woke up with a feeling of great urgency. She was sure he was in danger and that he wanted her to do something for him but she had no idea what it could be.

The next night she had the same dream again. Again she saw him standing at the bottom of that curious tower in that green light changing to blue; again he tried to make her understand what he was saying, but the heavy glass silence remained impenetrable. Before she woke up, however, it seemed as if his message had been brought back to two words: two words he kept on repeating time after time, forming them slowly, pleadingly with his lips. He was still repeating them when she woke up, without any idea of what he was trying to say.

During the month that followed she had the dream several times. It was always the same: the tower, the creeper, the green light, and silence, and Jan, weary and wounded, trying to make her understand two words only. And every time she woke up in tears, because she had no idea what they were.

The fortnight after she had dreamed the dream for the last time news came that Jan's ship was missing. People came to comfort her, but although she let them say what they wanted in order not to hurt their feelings, she didn't for a second believe that Jan was dead. He was standing somewhere at the bottom of a red tower in green sunlight calling her, and she would help him, if it would cost her everything she had.

But there was nothing she could do. She thought of boarding a ship to the East Indies but nobody knew exactly where the ship had got lost. She decided to remain where she was and wait until, somehow, they would be able to reach each other through the thick glass plate that separated them. She dreamed the dream many times after that and she began slowly to realize the first word was "your" and that the second word had an "o" in it; but she never found that second word.

Her waking life became less and less important to her. She would have wanted to sleep and dream forever, if there hadn't been hope that some day someone would come who would bring her news about Jan or his ship.

Every night she sat listening in the lamplight, knitting socks for him, alone in her little house; and whenever she heard the distant splash and rattle of an anchor dropping in the bay, she would put on her shawl and go out in the night and climb the dike to wait for the first boat coming ashore. Whatever the ship, she would invariably ask the same question: "Have you met the *Rising Hope*, the flag-ship of the East India Company?" The men in the boat would always be nice to her, for she was a pretty girl with the innocence of the faithful in her eyes. They would say: "Not that we know of, but we have passed so many ships in the distance which we didn't recognize that it's quite possible." Then she would ask: "Have you heard any news about Jan Viool, a sailor? He may have changed ships abroad." Then the men would get uncomfortable with pity and self-consciousness and say: "No."

This happened many times during the months that followed. She must have asked those questions on dozens of nights; misty, moonlit, stormy or rainy nights. She asked it in snow and hail, shouting against the gale or whispering in the summer breeze; but every time she got the same answer. She would always say: "Thank you, gentlemen," politely, and walk back along the dike: very pretty, very brave, and resume her knitting in the lamp-light, alone.

One night, almost a year after Jan had got lost, a night when there was no moon and no breeze and fog enclosed the Island of Schokland, she looked up in the lamplight, amazed, for she heard distinctly the splash and the rattle of an anchor dropping in the bay. That was very strange, for there was no wind and no visibility; the ships in the harbour were lying dead, the ropes silent against the masts, and everybody in the village was asleep in the comfortable certainty that no ship could reach the island that night.

She got up, put her shawl around her shoulders, went out and climbed the dike. She had been used to walking along it to the jetty, for that was where all boats moored, but the night was so thick with fog that she couldn't see one step in front of her, and so she stood still, listening.

She heard distinctly the creaking of oars approaching in the fog, the murmur of water against the bow of a boat, she even heard the oarsmen sighing and the soft clanking of the rudder chain, but she saw nothing. The sounds seemed to come straight at her, and for the first time since Jan had left she became conscious of being alone.

Then there was the scraping of an iron keel on the basalt of the dike, the rumbling of oars being pulled in, the splashing of people getting out and wading through the shallow water; then, suddenly, there came a faint light climbing towards her, with the scraping of hobnailed boots on the rocks.

The light came nearer and nearer, until she saw that it was a very old-fashioned lantern. Then it stood still, and the steps fell silent. She saw only that lantern, and nothing else; but she knew there must be men around it hidden in the fog, and she asked her question without seeing whom she was addressing.

"Have you met the *Rising Hope*, the flagship of the East India Company?" she asked, and for the first time she realized how often she had asked it before. The lantern shone motionlessly in the fog, and she was about to turn away when a voice said: "We have."

She took a long time asking her second question, for she had suddenly become afraid. This was the answer she had been waiting for, for almost a year; but now that she finally heard it a cold fear started creeping up her legs. "Have you heard any news about Jan Viool, a sailor?" she asked. "He may have changed ships abroad."

Again the lantern shone motionlessly in the fog for minutes on end, before the voice answered: "We have."

The fear had crept up so high now, that it nearly numbed her lips. "Do you know where he is?" she whispered.

Again the voice answered: "We do."

Then she asked her last question, and even before she had spoken she realized that it was going to decide her life. Asking that question was the bravest thing she had ever done; but as she had decided that she would help Jan even if it would cost everything she had, she looked at the motionless lantern bravely and said: "Could you take me to him?"

The silence that met her question lasted so long that she repeated it. Then the voice said: "We can. But it will cost you a lot."

"It doesn't matter," she said. "You can have anything I possess; tell me your price."

The voice answered: "It will cost you your soul."

And that was the moment she knew what had been the second word of the two Jan had tried to make her understand in all those dreams. It was "soul."

Mensje didn't hesitate; she didn't go back to her house to pack a bag or put on clogs; she went as she was: in her slippers, her shawl around her shoulders; the knitting needle, which she had stuck in her hair when she heard the

splash and rattle of the anchor dropping, went with her. The lantern guided her down the dike towards the sea, and she heard the splashing of boots in the water as the invisible men waded towards their invisible boat. Nobody offered to help her, so she put her slippers in her apron, gathered up her skirts, and waded after the lantern through the icy water. She saw the flank of a boat glistening in the fog, and had to climb into it unaided. The moment she sat down, dripping, on the middle bench, the oars rumbled out, the keel scraped free of the rocks, and the boat swung around in the darkness.

The lantern light had gone and she sat there quite alone shivering in the fog with the sound of oars ploughing the water all around her. She sat there for almost half an hour; then the lantern light flashed on again and she saw the dark, glistening wall of a big ship's side rising up beside her. A rope ladder was thrown down to her and she climbed it. The little swinging moon of the lantern followed her and made her climb into her own shadow.

She reached the rail, and climbed it, and stood on a vast

deserted deck. The lantern appeared beside her and the voice said: "Follow."

She was taken to a small cabin, that at first looked quite ordinary. The lantern was left with her, the voice said: "Go to sleep," and then there was the sound of a door shutting and of a key turning in the lock.

When she began to undress and put her shawl on the little stool in the cabin, she realized that it was not an ordinary cabin at all. When she tried to lift the stool, to put it nearer to the bunk, she couldn't move it because it was too heavy. It was made of stone. She looked around her at the small objects that had seemed so normal at first glance; they were all made either of lead or stone. When she had undressed and climbed into the bunk and tried to lift the blanket, she had to use both hands for it was a rug of closely knitted iron rings. She wriggled her way underneath it, and when she put her head on the pillow it felt hard and unyielding. It was filled with sand.

She lay on her back, gazing at the ceiling, getting colder and colder under the iron blanket and on the pillow of sand. She folded her hands to pray; but before her fingers had met she stopped and lay still, for there was no use any longer to pray for her soul. She shut her eyes and thought: good-bye life, good-bye sound of the wind in the drying nets, good-bye smell of freshly ironed aprons, good-bye Schokland, my home, good-bye.

She felt very sorry for herself when she thought that, but then an image dawned in the darkness of her closed eyes: a red tower, covered with unknown creeper, and a boy with a blood-soaked kerchief around his head calling her name. She smiled, because she realized that there was no point in saying good-bye to anything; her life was him. With that smile on her lips she fell asleep.

When she woke up again the lantern shone no more. The cabin was light: the curious blue-green light she knew so well from her dream. The first thing she saw gave her a shiver of terror: her hair seemed to be standing on end, it rose right to the ceiling and moved softly, waving about. She was so cold that it felt as if her body wasn't there any longer; when she swung the blanket aside it was much lighter than it had been the night before.

But she didn't notice this, for when she swung the blanket aside she saw a sight that nearly made her heart stop: the lower part of her body had changed into a glistening fishtail.

While she lay staring, aghast, at her scales and the forked fin that had once been her feet, a swift shadow passed above her. When she looked up she saw it was a little fish, that had swum in through the open porthole and now floated in the middle of the cabin. The little fish stared at her curiously out of the side of its head with one gold eye, then it turned, swam around the lantern, dived, and nibbled at her clothes. When she slowly stretched out her hand towards it, it flashed away, a streak of silver, and shot out of the porthole into the green light. She rose on her elbows and was amazed how light she was; then she looked out of the porthole and saw where she was.

The ship was lying in the deserted market place of a village of ruins. On the other side of the market place was a roofless church of red bricks, its tower broken; and the tower was covered with the curious creeper that she had never been able to recognize until this moment. It was seaweed.

She got out of the bunk, but never touched the floor, for she floated. Her tail was very strong; when she made a movement of walking she shot ahead and bumped her head against the wall, but her cry of pain was soundless. She understood that she was now in a world of gentle movements and silence.

She tried to open the door but found it was still locked; then she swung around and a quiver of her tail sent her soaring towards the porthole. She stretched her arms through it and tried to make her body follow, but the porthole was too narrow. Then she gave one strong sweep with her tail, and with a tearing pain she shot out into the green light, rose high up in the sky, turned, circled over the roofs of the ruins, and descended gently at the bottom of the broken tower, the very spot where Jan had stood.

While she hovered there sadly, looking around for her lost lover, an old man crossed the market place with slow long steps, rising into the air at each step as if he danced. She stirred her tail and flashed towards him so fast that she had to rise over his head and circle around before she cautiously descended beside him. He was a very old man with one eye and old-fashioned clothes; on the top of his bald head was a brand-mark of a skull and cross-bones, and she understood that he was a pirate. She had a moment of fear, but the thought that she could flash out of his reach with one sweep of her tail gave her a feeling of security. The old man didn't look a bit amazed on seeing her; his one eye gazed at her sadly, as if the sight of her filled him with pity.

She wondered how to communicate with him in this soundless world, but he took her head between his hands, pressed his cold lips against her ear and she heard a whisper. "Jan Viool has just left." Then the old man pointed at the green dusk behind the town, and moved his lips as if to say good-bye. She hesitated, for the dusk seemed to be filled with fear: slowly rising in blue circles, waving with the limp dead trees of seaweed, floating with the fleeting shadows of unseen fish. But she thought of Jan and his despair, swung her tail and shot away into the terror of that unknown world, her long hair streaming behind her, spurred by the one hope left to her: that one day, one night, she would find him.

She went from town to town. She had never known that the bottom of the sea was dotted with submerged villages and cities in which the drowned sailors waited for Judgment Day. She passed through scores of them and found that in every city there lived different people: Dutch, Norwegians, Greeks, Turks. There were cities entirely peopled by women, and villages in which only children lived. Everywhere along her way between the towns she found the silent wrecks of sunken ships, with weeds growing up their rigging and little fish playing around the mouths of their guns. It was the crews and the passengers of those sunken ships that peopled the ruins of the sunken towns.

But everywhere she arrived she got the same message whispered into her ear: "Jan Viool has just left," and every time the one who gave her that message, man, woman or child, pointed at the green dusk ahead of her.

She swam through the North Sea, the Gulf of Biscay, along the coast of Africa, until she arrived at a little village at the edge of a forest as dark as ink. The village was peopled with Portuguese fishermen, with rings in their ears, blue breeches, and long red caps on their heads with tassels which stretched out behind them when they walked with the long, dancing steps of the drowned. After one of these fishermen had taken her head between his hands again and whispered: "Jan Viool has just left," his hand rose slowly and pointed at the forest.

She wavered, for the darkness ahead of her looked so threatening that she couldn't find the courage to swing her tail and shoot into it. She looked around once more and saw the fisherman standing alone. When he saw her glancing back at him he took off his red cap and waved slowly a last good-bye.

The voyage through the forest lasted for weeks. It was so full of creeping fear and sudden streaks of terror that she got exhausted by darting aside all the time, away from the shadows that swooped down on her from the tangle of the high dead trees. The trees were peopled by monsters: sharks, inkfish, horrible crabs. They all attacked her: the sharks like streaks of white lightning, turning around on their backs as they swooped down, their white bellies flashing past her as she darted away from their terrible fangs in the nick of time; the inkfish spurting darkness, slowly slithering down the trees, their slimy tentacles groping for her in swirling clouds of ink; the crabs swinging out arms as derricks, with wide-open claws, snapping shut just behind her glistening, flickering tail.

When at last, exhausted, she reached the other side of the forest, she emerged into a desert overhung by solid green clouds. At first she had no idea where she was, but when she saw sticking out of the clouds the keels of ships, and hanging anchors slowly stirring in the circular tide, she understood that she was moving towards the centre of a sea of weeds called the Sargasso Sea.

She had often heard about this sea. Sailors said that all the wrecks of the ocean that did not sink were slowly dragged toward it, to end up in the weeds and join the ghostly fleet of barnacled hulks with broken masts covered with seaweed, slowly spinning around the centre of the Sargasso Sea which no human being had ever set eyes on.

She remembered that when she was still a child at school an old fisherman had once told them the story of how the Sargasso Sea came into being. Jesus, the old man had said, on finding out that the land was peopled with sinners, got so disgusted that He and His apostles boarded a ship called the *Aldebaran*. In it they sailed the seven seas for centuries, and whenever a ship was being drowned by a gale and battered by waves, there would at the ultimate moment appear a blue light on the horizon, and a cross would shine in the stormy darkness: the *Aldebaran*, coming to save them. But, so the old man had said, Jesus discovered in due course that the sailors were just as disgusting a crowd of sinners as the landlubbers had been. Hopeless and tired, He ordered His apostles to drop anchor in the loneliest spot of the Atlantic Ocean and wait there for Judgment Day. Like all ships lying still, the *Aldebaran* had started to grow weeds and barnacles. The weeds grew and grew, until they had completely overgrown the ship and covered the sea for miles around.

So when, on a dark green morning, she reached a rusty chain going straight up into the clouds of weeds, she hesitated for a while; but then she thought of Jan's desperate face, rose slowly along the chain and vanished in the clouds.

She seemed to rise through that swirling green mass of weeds for a very long time; then she saw a light overhead, a soft white glow like that of the sun hidden by the thin mist of a winter morning. She saw, as she got nearer, the bottom of an enormous ship, so overgrown with barnacles and mussels that it looked like the ceiling of a grotto that had been born when the world was very young. Somewhere among the rocks was a crack of light, and she swam towards it.

Amid the mussels and the barnacles she found after searching for a long time, a huge rusty iron ring, like a door knocker, and using all her strength she swung it to and fro until at last it knocked. There was a sound of heavy bolts, a creaking of huge hinges, and the crack got wider until a flat beam of golden light shone into the green darkness of the weeds like sunlight falling into a wood.

In that light she saw the face of a very old man with a white beard appear, and his blue innocent eyes gazed at her in amazement. He must be one of the apostles, and somehow she knew instantly that he was Peter. When she spoke she discovered that she had suddenly got her voice back; it sounded faint and distant, but it was unmistakably hers.

"Could you tell me," she asked, "where I can find Jan Viool, a sailor?"

"Who are you?" the old man asked gently.

"I am his girl," she said.

Old Peter looked at her intently, and then his face changed; as if only at that moment he realized that she was a mermaid.

"You are just a few days too late," he said. "He went back to the Island of Schokland the day before yesterday, alive again."

She felt a terrible sadness and at the same time a great joy overcame her, and when she repeated: "Alive!" she felt something warm go down her cheeks, the first warmth she had felt since she had woken up in that cabin of stone, long ago.

"Yes," said Peter, while shutting the door. "He has been lucky: some fool ashore has given up his soul for him."

She didn't know what to say any more. She saw, through her tears, the sunlight shrink to a vanishing crack; then it was dark again around her, and she sank slowly down along the chain until she was back in the desert, where the huge rusty blade of the anchor lay waiting to be lifted from the sand at Judgment Day.

She sat down on the anchor, and wept. She was quite alone. The thought of wandering among the drowned forever without even the hope of ever reaching the man she loved made her very sad, and for a while it seemed to her as if now there was nothing left to live for. But then she thought of his despair when he would arrive in the Island of Schokland and find her gone, and it was that thought that made her sweep her tail and shoot back into the horror of the black forest, across the nightmarish miles of sunken jungle, across ocean and seas, until at last she

reached the dike over which she saw the timid roofs of
Emmeloord peeping at the horizon.

On the dike stood a lonely man, staring sadly at the sea.
She rose from the waves and waved, but he didn't see her.
She called his name, but he didn't hear her. She pleaded,
shouted, jumped out of the water with a burst of silver
spray, lashing the waves with her tail; but he saw and heard
nothing. He sighed, and he turned slowly around, and
vanished behind the dike to go into the little house, in
which she knew he would lie down and dream of a girl,
standing at the foot of a broken red tower covered with
seaweed, smiling at him through a green glass plate, and
forming three small words with her lips which he would,
one night, perhaps understand.

Jan Viool became the lighthouse keeper of Schokland
and remained a brooder until the end of his life; but the
mermaid, who was immortal, realized in the end that all
men were brothers, and her love became like a fountain:
it shot up towards one sailor, but it rained down on all of
them. She remained in the sea around the Island of
Schokland until this day, and every time a storm is
brewing the fishermen hear a soft girl's voice, singing
above the murmur of the waves. When they hear it they
furl their sails, lock their cabins and go home to wait in
bed with their wives until the gale is over, which they
know will come before the dawn.

The Great Silkie of Sule Skerrie

ANON

This is a translation of an old ballad from the Isles of Orkney. Unfortunately it represents only a fragment of the whole. The original ballad tells how a young girl living in Norway falls in love with and has a child by a seal-man. Soon after the seal-man disappears. Seven years later he returns and fortells what the fate of his son and himself will be.

At the end of a further seven years the seal-man returns a second time and puts a gold chain round his son's neck. His son then follows him into the sea.

The girl, having lost her seal lover and seal son, marries again a "gunner good" who one day shoots two seals, an old one and a younger one. Round the neck of the younger seal there is a golden chain.

The rocky islands of Sule Skerrie (the skerries of the solen goose) lie twenty-five miles west of Hoy Head in the Orkneys and to this day are the homes of grey seals or selchies as they are called in the Orkneys.

An earthly nourris[1] sits and sings,
And aye she sings, "Ba, lily-wean,
Little ken I my bairnis' father,
Far less the land that he stops in."

Then one arose at her bed-foot,
An a grumly guest I'm sure was he;
"Here am I, thy bairnis' father,
Although that I be not comelie.

[1] *Nourris*, a nurse.

I am a man, upon the land,
An I am a silkie in the sea;
And when I'm far and far frae land,
My dwelling is in Sule Skerrie."

"It was na weel," quoth the maiden fair,
"It was na weel, indeed," quoth she,
"That the Great Silkie of Sule Skerrie
Should hae come and aught a bairn to me."

Now he has ta'en a purse of gold,
And he has put it upon her knee,
Saying, "Gie to me my little young son,
And take thee up thy nourris-fee.

An it shall come to pass on a summer's day,
When the sun shines hot on every stane,
That I will take my little young son,
And teach him for to swim the faem.

An thou shalt marry a proud gunner,
An a proud gunner I'm sure he'll be,
An the very first shot that e'er he shoots,
He'll shoot both my young son and me."

In the Kingdom of the Seals

DONALD A. MACKENZIE

THE sea fairies have grey skin-coverings and resemble seals. They dwell in cave houses on the borders of Land-under-Waves, where they have a kingdom of their own. They love music and the dance, like the green land fairies, and when harper or piper plays on the beach they come up to listen, their sloe-black eyes sparkling with joy. On moonlight nights they hear the mermaids singing on the rocks when human beings are fast asleep, and they call to them: "Sing again the old sea croons; sing again!" All night long the sea fairies call thus when mermaids cease to sing, and the mermaids sing again and again to them. When the wind pipes loud and free, and the sea leaps and whirls and swings and cries aloud with wintry merriment, the sea fairies dance with the dancing waves, tossing white petals of foam over their heads, and twining pearls of spray about their necks. They love to hunt the silvern salmon in the forests of seatangle and in ocean's deep blue glens, and far up dark ravines through which flow rivers of sweet mountain waters gemmed with stars.

The sea fairies have a language of their own, and they are also skilled in human speech. When they come ashore they can take the forms of men or women, and turn billows into dark horses with grey manes and long grey tails, and on these they ride over mountain and moor.

There was once a fisherman who visited the palace of the queen of sea fairies, and told on his return all he had heard. He dwelt in a little township nigh to John-o'-Groat's House, and was wont to catch fish and seals. When he found that he could earn much money by hunting seals, whose skins make warm winter clothing, he troubled little about catching salmon or cod, and worked constantly as a seal-hunter. He crept among the rocks searching for his prey, and visited lonely seal-haunted islands across the Pentland Firth, where he often found the strange sea-prowlers lying on smooth flat ledges of rock fast asleep in the warm sunshine.

In his house he had great bundles of dried sealskins, and people came from a distance to purchase them from him. His fame as a seal-hunter went far and wide.

One evening a dark stranger rode up to his house, mounted on a black, spirited mare with grey mane and grey tail. He called to the fisherman who came out, and then said: "Make haste and ride with me towards the east. My master desires to do business with you."

"I have no horse," the fisherman answered, "but I shall walk to your master's house on the morrow."

Said the stranger: "Come now. Ride with me. My good mare is fleet-footed and strong."

"As you will," answered the fisherman, who at once mounted the mare behind the stranger.

The mare turned round and right-about, and galloped eastward faster than the wind of March. Shingle rose in front of her like rock-strewn sea-spray, and a sand-cloud gathered and swept out behind like mountain mists that are scattered before a gale. The fisherman gasped for breath, for although the wind was blowing against his back when he mounted the mare, it blew fiercely in his face as he rode on. The mare went fast and far until she drew nigh to a precipice. Near the edge of it she halted suddenly. The fisherman found that the wind was still blowing seaward, although he had thought it had veered round as he rode. Never before had he sat on the back of so fleet-footed a mare.

Said the stranger: "We have almost reached my master's dwelling."

The fisherman looked round him with surprise, and saw neither house nor the smoke of one. "Where is your master?" he asked.

Said the stranger: "You shall see him presently. Come with me."

As he spoke he walked towards the edge of the precipice and looked over. The fisherman did the same, and saw nothing but the grey lonely sea heaving in a long slow swell, and sea-birds wheeling and sliding down the wind.

"Where is your master?" he asked once again.

With that the stranger suddenly clasped the seal-hunter in his arms, and crying, "Come with me," leapt over the edge of the precipice. The mare leapt with her master. Down, down they fell through the air, scattering the startled sea-birds. Screaming and fluttering, the birds rose in clouds about and above them, and down ever down the men and the mare continued to fall till they plunged into the sea, and sank and sank, while the light around them faded into darkness deeper than night. The fisherman wondered to find himself still alive as he passed through the sea depths, seeing naught, hearing naught, and still moving swiftly. At length he ceased to sink, and went forward. He suffered no pain or discomfort, nor was he afraid. His only feeling was of wonder, and in the thick, cool darkness he wondered greatly what would happen next. At length he saw a faint green light, and as he went onward the light grew brighter and brighter, until the glens and bens and forests of the sea kingdom rose before his eyes. Then he discovered that he was swimming beside the stranger and that they had both been changed into seals.

Said the stranger: "Yonder is my master's house."

The fisherman looked, and saw a township of foam-white houses on the edge of a great sea-forest and fronted by a bank of sea-moss which was green as grass but more beautiful, and very bright. There were crowds of seal-folk in the township. He saw them moving about to and fro, and heard their voices, but he could not understand their speech. Mothers nursed their babes, and young children played games on banks of green sea-moss, and from the brown and golden sea-forest came sounds of music and the shouts of dancers.

Said the stranger: "Here is my master's house. Let us enter."

He led the fisherman towards the door of a great foam-white palace with its many bright windows. It was thatched with red tangle, and the door was of green stone. The door opened as smoothly as a summer wave that moves across a river mouth, and the fisherman entered with his guide. He found himself in a dimly-lighted room, and saw an old grey seal stretched on a bed, and heard him moaning with pain. Beside the bed lay a blood-stained knife, and the fisherman knew at a glance that it was his own. Then he remembered that, not many hours before, he had stabbed a seal, and that it had escaped by plunging into the sea, carrying the knife in its back.

The fisherman was startled to realise that the old seal on the bed was the very one he had tried to kill, and his heart was filled with fear. He threw himself down and begged for forgiveness and mercy, for he feared he would be put to death.

The guide lifted up the knife and asked: "Have you ever seen this knife before?" He spoke in human language.

"That is my knife, alas!" exclaimed the fisherman.

Said the guide: "The wounded seal is my father. Our doctors are unable to cure him. They can do naught without your help. That is why I visited your house and urged you to come with me. I ask your pardon for deceiving you, O man! but as I love my father greatly, I had to do as I have done."

"Do not ask my pardon," the fisherman said; "I have need of yours. I am sorry and ashamed for having stabbed your father."

Said the guide: "Lay your hand on the wound and wish it to be healed,"

The fisherman laid his hand on the wound, and the pain that the seal suffered passed into his hand, but did not remain long. As if by magic, the wound was healed at once. Then the old grey seal rose up strong and well again.

Said the guide: "You have served us well this day, O man!"

When the fisherman entered the house, all the seals that were within were weeping tears of sorrow, but they ceased to weep as soon as he had laid his hand on the wound, and when the old seal rose up they all became merry and bright.

The fisherman wondered what would happen next. For a time the seals seemed to forget his presence, but at length his guide spoke to him and said: "Now, O man! you can return to your own home where your wife and children await you. I shall lead you through the sea-depths, and take you on my mare across the plain which we crossed when coming hither."

"I give you thanks," the fisherman exclaimed.

Said the guide: "Before you leave there is one thing you must do; you must take a vow never again to hunt seals."

The fisherman answered: "Surely, I promise never again to hunt for seals."

Said the guide: "If ever you break your promise you shall die. I counsel you to keep it, and as long as you do so you will prosper. Every time you set lines, or cast a net, you will catch much fish. Our seal-servants will help you, and if you wish to reward them for their services, take with you in your boat a harp or pipe and play sweet music, for music is the delight of all seals."

The fisherman vowed he would never break his promise, and the guide then led him back to dry land. As soon as he reached the shore he ceased to be a seal and became a man once again. The guide, who had also changed shape, breathed over a great wave and, immediately, it became a dark mare with a grey mane and grey tail. He then mounted the mare, and bade the fisherman mount behind him. The mare rose in the air as lightly as wind-tossed spray, and passing through the clouds of startled sea-birds reached the top of the precipice. On she raced at once, raising the shingle in front and a cloud of sand behind. The night was falling and the stars began to appear, but it was not quite dark when the fisherman's house was reached.

The fisherman dismounted, and his guide spoke and said: "Take this from me, and may you live happily." He handed the fisherman a small bag, and crying: "Farewell! Remember your vow," he wheeled his mare right round and passed swiftly out of sight.

The fisherman entered his house, and found his wife still there. "You have returned," she said. "How did you fare?"

"I know not yet," he answered. Then he sat down and opened the bag, and to his surprise and delight he found it was full of pearls.

His wife uttered a cry of wonder, and said: "From whom did you receive this treasure?"

The fisherman then related all that had taken place, and his wife wondered to hear him.

"Never again will I hunt seals," he exclaimed.

And he kept his word and prospered and lived happily until the day of his death.

Mermen

WILLIAM CRAIGIE

"Then Laughed the Merman"

THERE is an old Icelandic saying, frequently made use of, "Then laughed the merman," the origin of which is said to be as follows. Once a fisherman caught a merman and took it ashore with him; it had a big head and long arms, but resembled a seal from the waist downwards. The fisherman's young wife came down to the shore to meet him, and kissed and caressed him, at which the man was delighted and gave her great praise, while at the same time he struck his dog for fawning on him. Then laughed the merman, and the fisherman asked the reason why he did so. "At folly," said the merman. As the man went homewards, he stumbled and fell over a little mound, whereupon he cursed it, and wondered why it had ever been made upon his land. Then laughed the merman, saying, "Unwise is the man." The man kept the the merman prisoner for three nights, and during that time some pedlars came with their wares. The man had never been able to get shoes with soles as thick as he wished them, and although these merchants thought they had them of the best, yet of all their stock the man said they were too thin, and would soon wear through. Then laughed the merman, and said, "Many a man is mistaken that thinks himself wise." Neither by fair means nor foul could the man get any more out of him, except on the condition that he should be taken out again to the same fishing bank where he was caught; there he would squat on the blade of an outstretched oar, and answer all his questions, but not otherwise. The man took him out there, and after the merman had got out on the oar-blade, he asked him what the folly was that he laughed at, when he praised his wife and struck his dog. "At *your* folly, man," said the merman, "for your dog loves you as its own life, but your wife wishes you were dead. The knoll that you cursed is your treasure-mound, with wealth in plenty under it; so you were unwise in that, and therefore I laughed. The shoes will serve you all your life, for you have but three days to live."

With that the merman dived off the oar-blade, and so they parted, but everything turned out true that he had said.

> "Well I mind that morning
> The merman laughed so low;
> The wife to wait her husband
> To water's edge did go;
> She kissed him there so kindly,
> Though cold her heart as snow;
> He beat his dog so blindly,
> That barked its joy to show."

The Merman in the Faeroes

The merman is like a human being, but considerably smaller in growth, and with very long fingers. He lives at the bottom of the sea, and annoys fishers by biting the bait off the hooks and fixing these in the bottom, so that they have to cut the line. If he is caught, he is so dexterous that he can loose the thread that ties the hooks to the line, and so escape from being brought up, and taken on board like any other fish. One time when he tried to play his tricks at the bottom of the sea, he was rather unlucky, for just as he was about to lay hold of the line of Anfinn from Eldu-vik, with intent to make it fast, Anfinn gave a pull, and caught the merman by the right hand. With one hand he could not free himself from the line, and so was drawn up; a cross was made upon him, and he was taken home. Anfinn kept him in his house on the hearthstone, but had to remember every evening to make a cross on the four corners of this. He would eat nothing but fish-bait. When they went out to fish, they took the merman with them, and had to recollect to make the mark of the cross on him, when they took him on board the boat. When they rowed over a shoal of fish, he began to laugh and play in the boat, and they were sure of a good catch, if they put out their lines then, especially if he dipped his finger into the sea. Anfinn had the merman with him for a long time, but one day the sea was pretty stormy when they launched the boat, and they forgot to make the cross on him. When they had got out from land, he slipped overboard, and was never seen again.

The Fisher and the Merman

One cold winter day a fisherman had gone out to sea. It began to grow stormy when he was about to return, and he had trouble enough to clear himself. He then saw, near his boat, an old man with a long grey beard, riding on a wave. The fisherman knew well that it was the merman he saw before him, and knew also what it meant. "Uh, then, how cold it is!" said the merman as he sat and shivered, for he had lost one of his hose. The fisherman pulled off one of his, and threw it out to him. The merman disappeared with it, and the fisherman came safe to land. Some time after this the fisherman was again out at sea, far from land. All at once the merman stuck his head over the gunwale, and shouted out to the man in the boat,

"Hear, you man that gave the hose,
Take your boat and make for shore,
It thunders under Norway."

The fisherman made all the haste he could to get to land, and there came a storm the like of which had never been known, in which many were drowned at sea.

The Dead Merman and the Sand-Drift

A dead body was once washed ashore on the Danish coast, and buried in the churchyard of Nissum. No sooner had this been done than the sand began to blow over the country from the beach, and this continued for three days, growing always the longer the worse. People now began to think there was trolldom in the matter, and applied to a wise man for advice. On his learning that the sand-storm had begun immediately after the burial of the dead body from the sea, he declared that this was undoubtedly a merman, and that his burial in Christian ground had caused the drifting. They must instantly dig him up again, and see whether he had sucked his fore-finger into his mouth past the second joint. If he had done this there was no help for it, but if not they should bury him in the sand-hills, and the drifting would cease, They accordingly dug him up again, and sure enough they found him lying with his finger in his mouth, but he had got it no further than the second joint. They buried him in the sand-hills, and the drifting ceased. After that all bodies washed ashore were buried in these hills, down to quite recent times.

The Breton Mermaid

ONCE upon a time there was an old man who lived with his wife in a hut by the sea. The old man made wooden shoes, or sabots as they are called in Brittany, which were the only kind that the poor fishermen who were his customers could afford. He, too, was very poor, and he was always glad when his children, a boy and a girl, brought home something from the seashore that they could eat.

One day as the children were searching the beach they saw a mermaid swimming nearby, singing sweetly and shedding a golden radiance on the waters. The children ran home to tell their father about the wonderful golden fish they had seen in the bay.

The shoemaker was determined to catch such an exotic creature, so he hurried down to the shore, baited his fishing lines, and waited. But the mermaid would not touch the bait, and was clearly not to be caught that way.

The shoemaker was at a loss what to do next until one day, by a lucky chance, he saw the mermaid asleep on the calm sea. Wading out with a large basket he passed it beneath the mermaid and managed to carry her, still sleeping, to the shore. She seemed to be a beautiful young girl of about eighteen with golden hair, a white shining body and a glittery fish-tail. Just then the mermaid awoke and was terrified to find herself a prisoner on land. In the sweetest tones she implored the shoemaker to take her back to sea.

35

"No," he answered, "we have all waited so long to catch you that I am going to carry you to my house so all my family can see you. When you have sung us a song I will take you back to the water—if my wife agrees."

But when the shoemaker showed the mermaid to his wife she was not at all willing to let her go and said in a most unfeeling way: "No, it is a splendid fish. I have never seen one like it. We will have it for supper."

"Alas!" cried the mermaid," if you do you will never eat again. Ask for anything you like and I will grant it you, for I have the same powers as the fairies; but do please carry me back to the sea for I am growing weaker and weaker and I shall soon die if I stay on land."

At this the woman relented and taking one handle of the basket and her husband the other they hurried back to the shore where the sea soon revived the mermaid so that she began to laugh with joy at her escape.

"What do you wish for?" asked the grateful mermaid of the shoemaker.

"Bread and fish and clothes for my wife, my children and myself," answered the man.

"You shall have all you want in twenty-four hours," said the mermaid, "but is there nothing more you would like?"

"I should like a little ready cash to pay my debts and buy one or two things," replied the shoemaker.

The mermaid said nothing but began to beat the water with her tail and all the droplets that splashed on to the sand at the shoemaker's feet immediately turned into gold pieces! The shoemaker and his wife were amazed and thanked the mermaid with all their hearts.

"Come back to the same place in twenty-four hours," said the mermaid and she swam away with a last flick of

her tail that sent another shower of gold to the shoemaker's feet.

When the twenty-four hours had elapsed the shoemaker
went to the shore and there was the mermaid waiting for
him. When she saw him she beat the waves with her tail
and sang a sweet song and in a moment a large wave
rolled to the shore bringing with it a huge chest.

"You will find there all the clothes you need," said the
friendly mermaid, "and when you need fish just come to
the shore."

Again the shoemaker and his wife thanked the mermaid and then with some difficulty they dragged the chest home. When they opened it they found it full of beautiful clothes and when they tried them on they all fitted perfectly!

After this whenever they needed fish the children had only to go to the shore to return in a few minutes laden with as many fish as they could carry.

Only once more did the mermaid appear to them and this time too they were enriched by a shower of gold, then she bade them farewell forever, telling them she was going a long journey back home to India.

Naturally the shoemaker and his family lived happily ever after.

Andromeda

CHARLES KINGSLEY

The Andromeda legend is part of the story of the Greek hero, Perseus, who, with the help of Pallas Athené, slew the Gorgon Medusa, the monster whose look was so terrible that it turned men to stone.

On his way home Perseus flew on his winged sandals over the coast of Ethiopia and there he saw Andromeda.

The custom of offering a human sacrifice to the sea-gods to propitiate them and ensure that the fertility of the waters was maintained was common among the ancestors of the Greeks.

AND Perseus flew along the shore above the sea; and he went on all the day, and the sky was black with smoke; and he went on all the night, and the sky was red with flame.

And at the dawn of day he looked toward the cliffs; and at the water's edge, under a black rock, he saw a white image stand.

"This," thought he, "must surely be the statue of some sea-God; I will go near and see what kind of Gods these barbarians worship."

So he came near; but when he came, it was no statue, but a maiden of flesh and blood; for he could see her tresses streaming in the breeze; and as he came closer still, he could see how she shrank and shivered, when the waves sprinkled her with cold salt spray. Her arms were spread above her head, and fastened to the rock with chains of brass; and her head drooped on her bosom, either with sleep, or weariness, or grief. But now and then she looked up and wailed, and called her mother; yet she did not see Perseus, for the cap of darkness was on his head.

Full of pity and indignation, Perseus drew near and looked upon the maid. Her cheeks were darker than his were, and her hair was blue-black like a hyacinth: but Perseus thought—"I have never seen so beautiful a maiden; no, not in all our Isles. Surely, she is a king's daughter. Do barbarians treat their king's daughters thus? She is too fair, at least to have done any wrong. I will speak to her."

And lifting the hat from his head, he flashed into her sight. She shrieked with terror, and tried to hide her face with her hair, for she could not with her hands; but Perseus cried,—

"Do not fear me, fair one; I am a Hellen, and no barbarian. What cruel men have bound you? But first I will set you free."

And he tore at the fetters; but they were too strong for him; the maiden cried—

"Touch me not; I am accursed, devoted as a victim to sea-Gods. They will slay you, if you dare set me free."

"Let them try," said Perseus; and drawing Herpé from his thigh, he cut through the brass as if it had been flax.

"Now," he said, "you belong to me, and not to these sea-Gods, whosoever they may be!" But she only called the more on her mother.

"Why call on your mother? She can be no mother to have left you here. If a bird is dropped out of the nest, it belongs to the man who picks it up. If a jewel is cast by the wayside, it is his who dare win it and wear it, as I will wear you. I know now why Pallas Athené sent me hither. She sent me to gain a prize worth all my toil and more."

And he clasped her in his arms, and cried—"Where are these sea-Gods, cruel and unjust, who doom fair maids to death? I carry the weapons of Immortals. Let them measure their strength against mine! But tell me, maiden, who you are, and what dark fate brought you here?"

And she answered, weeping—

"I am the daughter of Cepheus, King of Iopa, and my mother is Cassiopœia of the beautiful tresses, and they called me Andromeda, as long as life was mine. And I stand bound here, hapless that I am, for the sea-monster's food, to atone my mother's sin. For she boasted of me once that I was fairer than Atergatis, Queen of the Fishes; so she in her wrath sent the sea-floods, and her brother the Fire King sent the earthquakes, and wasted all the land, and after the floods a monster bred of the slime, who devours all living things. And now he must devour me, guiltless though I am—me who never harmed a living thing, nor saw a fish upon the shore but I gave it life, and threw it back into the sea; for in our land we eat no fish, for fear of Atergatis their Queen. Yet the priests say that nothing but my blood can atone for a sin which I never committed."

But Perseus laughed, and said—"A sea-monster? I have fought with worse than him: I would have faced Immortals for your sake; how much more a beast of the sea?"

Then Andromeda looked up at him, and new hope was kindled in her breast, so proud and fair did he stand, with one hand round her, and in the other the glittering sword. But she only sighed, and wept the more, and cried,—

"Why will you die, young as you are? Is there not death and sorrow enough in the world already? It is noble for me to die, that I may save the lives of a whole people; but you, better than them all, why should I slay you too? Go you your way; I must go mine."

But Perseus cried—"Not so; for the Lords of Olympus, whom I serve, are the friends of the heroes, and help them on to noble deeds. Led by them, I slew the Gorgon, the beautiful horror; and not without them do I come hither, to slay this monster with that same Gorgon's head. Yet hide your eyes when I leave you, lest the sight of it freeze you too to stone."

But the maiden answered nothing, for she could not believe his words. And then, suddenly looking up, she pointed to the sea, and shrieked,—

"There he comes, with the sunrise, as they promised. I must die now. How shall I endure it? Oh, go! Is it not dreadful enough to be torn piecemeal, without having you to look on?" And she tried to thrust him away.

But he said—"I go: yet promise me one thing ere I go; that if I slay this beast you will be my wife, and come back with me to my kingdom in fruitful Argos, for I am a king's heir. Promise me, and seal it with a kiss."

Then she lifted up her face, and kissed him; and Perseus laughed for joy, and flew upward, while Andromeda crouched trembling on the rock, waiting for what might befall.

On came the great sea-monster, coasting along like a huge black galley, lazily breasting the ripple, and stopping at times by creek or headland, to watch for the laughter of girls at their bleaching, or cattle pawing on the sand hills, or boys bathing on the beach. His great sides were fringed

with clustering shells and sea-weeds, and the water gurgled in and out of his wide jaws, as he rolled along, dripping and glistening, in the beams of the morning sun.

At last he saw Andromeda, and shot forward to take his prey, while the waves foamed white behind him the fish fled leaping.

Then down from the height of the air fell Perseus like a shooting star; down to the crests of the waves, while Andromeda hid her face as he shouted; and then there was silence for a while.

At last she looked up trembling, and saw Perseus springing toward her; and instead of the monster a long black rock, with the sea rippling quietly round it.

Who then so proud as Perseus, as he leapt back to the rock, and lifted his fair Andromeda in his arms, and flew with her to the cliff-top, as a falcon carries a dove?

Who so proud as Perseus, and who so joyful as all the Æthiop people? For they had stood watching the monster from the cliffs, wailing for the maiden's fate. And already a messenger had gone to Cepheus and Cassiopœia, where they sat in sackcloth and ashes on the ground, in the innermost palace chambers, awaiting their daughter's end. And they came, and all the city with them, to see the wonder, with songs and dances, with cymbals and harps, and received their daughter back again, as one alive from the dead.

Then Cepheus said—"Hero of the Hellens, stay here with me and be my son-in-law, and I will give you the half of my kingdom."

"I will be your son-in-law," said Perseus, "but of your kingdom I will have none; for I long after the pleasant land of Greece, and my mother who waits for me at home."

Then Cepheus said—"You must not take my daughter away at once, for she is to us like one alive from the dead. Stay with us here a year, and after that you shall return with honour." And Perseus consented; but before he went to the palace, he bade the people bring stones and wood, and built three altars, one to Athené, and one to Hermes, and one to Father Zeus, and offered bullocks and rams.

Thor and the Midgard Serpent

In Norse mythology the earth was represented as a disc entirely surrounded by water—the ocean. In the ocean lived the Midgard serpent a monster so gigantic that its coils stretched right round the world so that its head and tail nearly met.

Thor (from whose name Thursday is derived) was one of the most popular of the Norse gods. He was an imposing figure distinguished by his red beard and stentorian voice and by the mighty stone hammer he always carried. Like all Norse heroes Thor could never resist a challenge, but in undertaking to fight the Midgard serpent he almost bit off more than he could chew!

ONE day Thor set out to fish for the Midgard serpent that lies in the depths of the ocean encircling the whole world, with its head and tail almost, but not quite, meeting.

Thor went alone, disguised as a young man. That same evening he came to the home of a giant called Hymer and there he stayed the night.

The next morning Hymer got up and began to get his boat ready for a day's fishing. Seeing this, Thor sprang up and asked if he could go. Hymer said that a slip of a lad was not much use to him, and he added: "I am going far out to sea and I shall stay there a long time. If you come with me, you are sure to catch cold."

Thor answered that he was capable of rowing quite as far as the giant and it remained to be seen who would be first to want to row back. He became so furious that he nearly set Hymer's head ringing with his hammer, but managed to restrain himself in time, for he meant to save his strength for the serpent.

Thor then asked Hymer what they should use as bait, but the giant merely told him to find his own. So Thor turned to where a herd of oxen, belonging to Hymer, was grazing, and taking the biggest of the oxen he struck off its head and took it down to the shore. Hymer had already launched the boat, so Thor stepped aboard and sitting down in the stern took up a pair of oars and began to row. Hymer had to admit that the boat made good progress with Thor rowing, and with both of them at the oars they soon reached the banks where Hymer was accustomed to sit and catch flat fish. But Thor wanted to go further out so they had another spell of hard rowing. At last Hymer said they had rowed so far out that it would be dangerous to go further, because of the Midgard Serpent. But Thor insisted that they should carry on rowing and did so, which made the giant very angry.

When at last they had shipped oars, Thor got ready a very strong line with a no less powerful hook and baited the hook with the ox-head. Then he threw the ox-head overboard and it sank to the bottom of the sea.

The Midgard Serpent went to swallow the bait and the hook stuck fast in the roof of its mouth. Then the serpent tugged so hard that Thor's knuckles were cracked against the boat's gunwale. At this Thor became angry and using every ounce of strength he braced himself so hard that his legs went straight through the bottom of the boat and his feet were pressed against the sea bed.

Slowly Thor pulled the serpent up to the boat and never was there a more terrible sight than Thor with his eyes fixed grimly on the serpent and the serpent glaring back and vomiting poison.

Then Hymer turned ashen with fear when he saw the serpent and the sea pouring into his boat. At the very moment that Thor grasped his hammer and raised it, Hymer fumbled for his knife and cut off Thor's line at the gunwale so that the serpent sank back into the sea. Thor flung his hammer at the serpent and some say he struck off its head, but others believe the Midgard Serpent still lives lying at the bottom of the ocean. Thor clenched his fist and gave Hymer a box on the ear that knocked him overboard. Then he waded ashore.

The Kraken

ALFRED LORD TENNYSON

Sailors greatly feared this legendary monster which was believed to wrap its tentacles round ships and drag them to the bottom of the sea. The Kraken is first mentioned by name in Bishop Pontoppidan's The Natural History of Norway *(1752–3). Pontoppidan says that the monster is so big that it looks like a group of floating islands. The tentacles, or arms as Pontoppidan calls them, "stand up as high and large as the masts of a medium sized vessel". In his book* In the Wake of the Sea Serpent *Bernard Heuvelmans identifies the Kraken with the giant squid.*

Below the thunders of the upper deep;
Far, far beneath in the abysmal sea,
His ancient, dreamless, uninvaded sleep
The Kraken sleepeth: faintest sunlights flee
About his shadowy sides: above him swell
Huge sponges of millennial growth and height;
And far away into the sickly light,
From many a wondrous grot and secret cell
Unnumber'd and enormous polypi
Winnow with giant arms the slumbering green.
There hath he lain for ages and will lie
Battening upon huge seaworms in his sleep,
Until the latter fire shall heat the deep;
Then once by man and angels to be seen,
In roaring he shall rise and on the surface die.

The Great Island Fish

SIR RICHARD BURTON

The Great Island Fish is a favourite monster of legend and is to be found in many ancient sources apart from The Arabian Nights, *from which this extract is taken. He even turns up in a famous passage from* Paradise Lost *(Book I, lines 200–9) where Milton confuses him with the Biblical Leviathan, presumably on account of his size.*

Docile by nature, this amiable monster suffers many indignities at the hands of unsuspecting sailors who mistake his enormous back for dry land. Sinbad the Sailor's experience is typical.

MY father was a merchant, one of the notables of my native place, a monied man and ample of means, who died whilst I was yet a child, leaving me much wealth in money and lands and farm houses. When I grew up, I laid hands on the whole and ate the best and drank freely and wore rich clothes and lived lavishly, companioning and consorting with youths of my own age, and considering that this course of life would continue for ever and ken no change. Thus did I for a long time, but at last I awoke from my heedlessness and, returning to my senses, I found my wealth had become unwealth and my condition ill-conditioned and all I once hent had left my hand. And recovering my reason I was stricken with dismay and confusion and bethought me of a saying of our lord Solomon, son of David (on whom be peace!), which I had heard aforetime from my father, "Three things are better than other three; the day of death is better than the day of birth, a live dog is better than a dead lion and the grave is better than want." Then I got together my remains of estates and property and sold all, even my clothes, for three thousand dirhams, with which I resolved to travel to foreign parts.

So taking heart I bought me goods, merchandise and all needed for a voyage and, impatient to be at sea, I embarked, with a company of merchants, on board a ship bound for Bassorah. There we again embarked and sailed many nights, and we passed from isle to isle and sea to sea and shore to shore, buying and selling and bartering everywhere the ship touched, and continued our course till we came to an island as it were a garth of the gardens of Paradise. Here the captain cast anchor and making fast to the shore, put out the landing planks. So all on board landed and made furnaces and lighting fires therein, busied themselves in various ways, some cooking and some washing, whilst other some walked about the island for solace, and the crew fell to eating and drinking and playing and sporting. I was one of the walkers but, as we were thus engaged, behold the master who was standing on the gunwale cried out to us at the top of his voice, saying, "Ho there! passengers, run for your lives and hasten back to the ship and leave your gear and save yourselves from destruction. Allah preserve you! For this island whereon ye stand is no true island, but a great fish stationary a-middlemost of the sea, whereon the sand hath settled and trees have sprung up of old time, so that it is become like unto an island; but, when ye lighted fires on it, it felt the heat and moved; and in a moment it will sink with you into the sea and ye will all be drowned. So leave your gear and seek your safety ere ye die!" All who heard him

left gear and goods, clothes washed and unwashed, fire pots and brass cooking-pots, and fled back to the ship for their lives, and some reached it while others (amongst whom was I) did not, for suddenly the island shook and sank into the deep, with all that were thereon, and the dashing sea surged over it with clashing waves. I sank with the others down, down into the deep, but Almighty Allah preserved me from drowning and threw in my way a great wooden tub of those that had served the ship's company for tubbing. I gripped it for the sweetness of life and, bestriding it like one riding, paddled with my feet like oars, whilst the waves tossed me as in sport right and left. Meanwhile the captain made sail and departed with those who had reached the ship, regardless of the

drowning and the drowned; and I ceased not following
the vessel with my eyes, till she was hid from sight and I
made sure of death. Darkness closed in upon me while in
this plight and the winds and waves bore me on all that
night and the next day, till the tub brought to with me
under the lee of a lofty island, with trees overhanging the
tide. I caught hold of a branch and by its aid clambered up
on to the land, after coming nigh upon death; but when I
reached the shore, I found my legs cramped and numbed
and my feet bore traces of the nibbling of fish upon their
soles; withal I had felt nothing for excess of anguish and
fatigue. I threw myself down on the island-ground, like
a dead man, and drowned in desolation, swooned away.

The Man Whale

JÓN ARNASON

IN ancient times, in the south part of Iceland it was the custom to go in a boat, at a certain season of the year, from the mainland to the cliffs, Geirfuglasker, to procure sea-birds and the eggs which they were in the habit of laying there. The passage to these rocks was always looked upon as an unsafe one, as they stood some way out at sea, and a constant and heavy surf beat upon them.

It happened once that some men went thither in a boat at the proper season for the purpose, as the weather seemed to promise a long calm. When they arrived at the rocks, some of them landed, the rest being left to take care of the boat. Suddenly a heavy wind came on, and the latter were forced to leave the island in haste, as the sea became dangerous and the surf beat furiously upon the cliffs. All those who had landed were enabled to reach the boat in time, at the signal from their companions, except one, a young active man, who, having gone in his zeal higher and farther than the others, was longer in getting down to the beach again. By the time he did get down, the waves were so high, that though those in the boat wrought their best to save him, they could not get near enough to him, and so were compelled for their own lives' sake to row to shore. They determined, however, when the storm should

54

abate its fury, to return to the rocks and rescue him, knowing that unless they did so and the wind were soon spent, the youth could not but perish from cold and hunger. Often they tried to row to the Geirfuglasker, but, the whole season through, they were unable to approach them, as the wind and surf always drove them back. At last, deeming the young man dead, they gave up the attempt and ceased to risk their lives in seas so wrathful.

So time passed away, until the next season for seeking sea-birds came round, and the weather being now calm, the peasants embarked in their boat for the Geirfuglasker. When they landed upon the cliffs, great was their astonishment at seeing come towards them a man, for they thought that no one could live in so wild and waste a spot. When the man drew near them, and they recognized him as the youth who had been left there the year before, and whom they had long ago given up as lost, their wonder knew no bounds, and they guessed that he had the elves to thank for his safety. They asked him all sorts of questions. What had he lived upon? Where had he slept at night? What had he done for fire in the winter? and so forth, but he would give them none but vague replies, which left them just as wise as they were before. He said, however, he had never once left the cliff, and that he had been very comfortable there, wanting for nothing. They then rowed him to land, where all his friends and kin received him with unbounded amazement and joy, but, question him as they would, could get but mighty little out of him concerning his life on the cliffs the whole year through. With time, the strangeness of this event and the wonder it had awakened passed away from men's minds, and it was little if at all more spoken of.

One Sunday in the summer, certain things that took

place in the church at Hvalsnes filled people with astonishment. There were large numbers there, and among them the young man who had passed a year on the cliffs of the Geirfuglasker. When the service was over and the folk began to leave the church, what should they find standing in the porch but a beautiful cradle with a baby in it. The coverlet was richly embroidered, and wrought of a stuff that nobody had ever seen before. But the strangest part of the business was, that though everybody looked at the cradle and child, nobody claimed either one or the other, or seemed to know anything whatever about them. Last of all came the priest out of church, who, after he had admired and wondered at the cradle and child as much as the others, asked whether there was no one present to whom they belonged. No one answered. Then he asked whether there was no one present who had enough interest in the child to desire him to baptize it. No one either answered or came forward.

At this moment the priest happened to cast his eyes on the young peasant, concerning whose sojourn on the Geirfuglasker rocks he had always felt particularly suspicious, and calling him aside, asked him whether he had any idea who its father was, and whether he would like the child baptized. But the youth turning angrily from him declared that he knew nothing whatever about the child or its father.

"What care I," he said, "whether you baptize the child or no? Christen it or drown it, just which you think fit; neither it, nor its father, nor its mother, are aught to me."

As these words left his lips, there suddenly appeared in the porch a woman, handsomely apparelled, of great beauty and noble stature, whom no one had ever seen before. She snatched the coverlet from the cradle, and flinging it in through the door of the church, said:

"Be witnesses all, that I wish not the church to lose its dues for this child's baptism."

Then turning to the young peasant, and stretching out her hands towards him, she cried, "But thou, O faithless coward, disowner of thy child, shalt become a whale, the fiercest and most dreaded in the whole wide sea!"

With these words, she seized the cradle and disappeared.

The priest, however, took the coverlet which she had flung into the church, and made of it an altar-cloth, the handsomest that had ever been seen. As for the young peasant, he went mad on the spot; and, rushing down to the Holmur Cliffs, which rise sheer from the deep water, made as if he would throw himself from them. But while he hesitated for a moment on the brink, lo! a fearful change came over him, and he began to swell to a vast size, till, at last, he became so large, that the rock could no longer bear him, but crumbling beneath him hurled him into the sea. There he was changed into a great whale, and the red cap which he had been wearing, became a red head.

After this, his mother confessed that her son had spent the year with the elves upon the Geirfuglasker. On his being left on the rocks by his companions (so he had declared to her), he had at first wandered about in despair, filled only with the thought of throwing himself into the waves to die a speedy death rather than suffer all the pangs of hunger and cold; but a lovely girl had come to him, and telling him she was an elf, had asked him to spend the winter with her. She had borne him a child before the end of the year, and only allowed him to go to shore when his companions came again to the cliffs, on condition that he would have this child baptized when he should find it in

the church-porch, threatening him, if he failed in the fulfilment of this, with the severest punishment and most hapless fate.

Now Redhead, the whale, took up his abode in the Faxafjord, and wrought mischief there without end, destroying boats innumerable, and drowning all their crews, so that at last it became unsafe to cross any part of the bay, and nothing could either prevent his ravages or drive him away. After matters had gone on like this for some time, the whale began to haunt a narrow gulf between Akranes and Kjarlanes, which is now called after him, Hvalfjördur.

At that time there lived at Saurboer, in Hvalfjardarströnd, an aged priest, who, though hale and hearty, was blind. He had two sons and a daughter, who were all in the flower of their youth, and who were their father's hope and stay, and, as it were, the very apple of his eye. His sons were in the habit of fishing in Hvalfjördur, and one day when they were out they encountered the whale,

Redhead, who overthrew their boat and drowned them both. When their father heard of their death, and how it had been brought about, he was filled with grief, but uttered not a word at the time.

Now it must be known that this old priest was well skilled in all magical arts.

Not long after this, one fine morning in the summer, he bade his daughter take his hand and guide him down to the sea-shore. When he arrived there, he planted the end of the staff which he had brought with him, in the waves, and leaning on the handle fell into deep thought.

After a few minutes he asked his daughter, "How looks the sea?"

She answered, "My father, it is as bright and smooth as a mirror."

Again, a few minutes, and he repeated, "How looks the sea?"

She replied, "I see on the horizon a black line, which draws nearer and nearer, as it were a shoal of whales, swimming quickly into the bay."

When the old man heard that the black line was approaching them, he bade the girl lead him along the shore towards the inland end of the bay. She did so, and the black surging sea followed them constantly. But as the water became shallower, the girl saw that the foam arose, not from a shoal of whales, as she had thought at first, but from the swimming of a single huge whale with a red head, who came rapidly towards them along the middle of the bay, as if drawn to them by some unseen power. A river ran into the extreme end of the gulf, and the old priest begged his daughter to lead him still on along its banks. As they went slowly up the stream, the old man feeling every footstep before him, the whale followed them, with a heavy struggle, as the river contained but little water for so vast a monster to swim in. Yet forward they went, and the whale still after them, till the river became so narrow between its high walls of rock, that the ground beneath their feet quaked as the whale followed them. After a while they came to a waterfall, up which the monster leaped with a spring that made the land tremble far and wide, and the very rocks totter. But they came at last to a lake, from which the river rose, whose course they had followed from the sea; the lake Hvalvatn. Here the heart of the monster broke from very toil and anguish, and he disappeared from their eyes.

When the old priest returned home, after having charmed the whale thus to his death, all the people from far and near thanked him for having rid their coasts of so dread a plague.

And in case anybody should doubt the truth of this story of Redhead, the man-whale, we may as well say that on the shores of the lake Hvalvatn, mighty whale-bones were found lying long after the date of this tale.

Inside the Monster

LUCIAN OF SAMOTHRACE

The following extract is taken from The True History *by Lucian of Samo-thrace, a Greek satirist who lived in the second century A.D. Although not strictly a sea-legend it is easily the most entertaining example I have come across of the* Jonah and the Whale *myth where the hero (heroes in this case) is swallowed by a sea-monster.*

The True History *is a work which has more in common with Baron Munchausen than anything else. In his Introduction Lucian tells us that, although he doesn't mind travel writers telling tall stories, he does object to them expecting to be believed. For himself: "My subject is then what I have neither seen, experienced, nor been told; what neither exists nor could by any stretch of the imagination do so. I humbly solicit my readers' incredulity."*

The story begins when Lucian sets sail with fifty companions from the Pillars of Hercules into the Atlantic on a voyage of discovery. Almost immediately his ship encounters a water-spout which sweeps it 350 miles into the air to the Kingdom of the moon. After many adventures the ship at last begins to descend gradually down to the sea once more. . . .

TOWARDS noon on the fourth day the wind died away and we were gently set down on the sea. Our delight at finding ourselves afloat is indescribable; overjoyed at our good fortune we dived overboard and swam, the sea being calm and the weather good. But alas, so often a change for the better only heralds the start of fresh troubles! For after sailing another two days, at sunrise on the third we saw a school of whales and sea monsters. Among them was one much bigger than all the rest—at least two hundred miles in length. It swam towards us with its mouth gaping open, churning the sea into foam for miles all around and displaying the most enormous pointed teeth the size of tree trunks.

We embraced each other for the last time and awaited our fate. The monster was on us immediately and swallowed us up, ship and all. By good fortune we escaped being crushed, the ship slipping through a gap between the teeth.

At first all was dark within and we could see nothing, but the next time the monster opened its mouth we saw an enormous cavern big enough to contain a city of ten thousand people. All about us were small fish, the broken remains of all kinds of animals, the masts of ships, anchors, human bones and debris of every sort. In the centre of the whale was a range of small hills formed so far as we could tell from the enormous quantities of mud that the monster had swallowed. Trees of all kinds grew there as well as vegetables—the latter showing every sign of having been cultivated and sea-birds of many kinds nested in the trees.

For a while we wept but at last I roused the crew and set them making the ship fast and starting a fire. Then we prepared our supper, for there was an abundance of fish on all sides. Next day we kept watch and whenever the whale opened his mouth we caught sight of land, or mountains, or sometimes of the sky only or quite often of islands; so we knew that the monster was swimming at a great rate to all quarters of the ocean. At last we grew tired of keeping watch so I took seven of my ship's company and set off into the forest to see what we could find. We had scarcely gone half a mile when we found a temple which by its inscription proved to have been dedicated to Poseidon. Nearby we saw many graves with

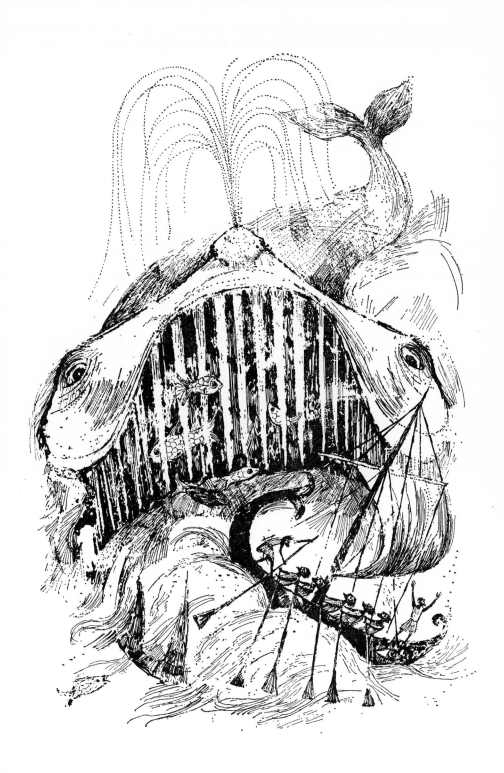

columns placed on them and close by a fresh water spring. We also heard the barking of a dog and saw smoke in the distance which lead us to believe that there must be houses nearby.

Hastening forward we encountered an old man and a youth who were busy making a garden, channelling water to it from the spring. We stood there filled with conflicting feelings of joy and fear. They no doubt felt the same way. For a long time no one spoke. At last the old man said; "Who are you, strangers? Are you sea spirits or just unlucky mortals like us? For our part, we are men, born and bred on land but now condemned to captivity inside this monster, hardly knowing whether we are alive or dead."

I answered: "Father, we are also men. We arrived here only yesterday when our ship was swallowed up whole. We set out to explore the forest and some heavenly guide has led us to you so that we should find out that we are not the only men imprisoned inside this monster. Please tell us your story, who you are and how you came here."

The old man answered that first we must eat, and so saying he brought us to his house and set before us a meal of greens, nuts and fish, together with wine. The house was small but adequately furnished for their needs. The meal finished he asked to hear our adventures. I told him everything that had happened right up to our being swallowed by the monster.

The old man was amazed but afterwards he told his own story: "My friends, I am a native of Cyprus and a merchant. I set out on a trading voyage with my son and a number of friends, bound for Italy. I had a noble ship full of valuable cargo. Perhaps you have noticed the wreckage in the whale's mouth. We had fair weather as far as Sicily, but there we were caught in such a terrific storm that we drove before it for three days out into the Atlantic where it was our misfortune to meet the whale, which swallowed us up; we two alone survived, the rest we buried here building a temple to Poseidon. Since then we have lived like this tending our garden and living on fish and nuts. We have all the wood we need, as you can see, and there are vines here too which yield the finest wines. The spring gives us the purest stone cold water; we make our bed of leaves, burn as much wood as we like for our fire, hunt wild birds and catch fish by going out on to the monster's gills; if we wish to bathe there is a salt lake quite near, two or three miles round and stocked full of all kinds of fish. Here we can swim or sail in a little boat I built myself. We have been here twenty-seven years. Our existence might have been bearable if it were not for our hostile neighbours; an unfriendly troublesome lot."

"Indeed," said I, "so there are others living here besides yourselves?"

"A great many," he replied, "but they are unfriendly to strangers and hideous to look at.

"The western side of the forest is held by the Tarychanians: they have eel's eyes and the faces of lobsters, are fierce and warlike and live on raw fish. The right hand side of the cavern belongs to the Tritonomendetes who are human from the waist upwards but weasels below. They are not quite so obnoxious as the rest. The left is the territory of the Carcinochirians and the Thinocephalians who are allies. The land between is inhabited by the Pagurodians and the Psittopodians who are savage and very fleet of foot. The eastern region near the monster's mouth is for the most part desert, as a result of constantly

being flooded with salt water. I lease it from the Psittopodians with an annual payment of five hundred oysters.

"That is how the land is divided up and now it is up to
you to decide whether we can make a stand against these
tribes or if not how we can live safely amongst them."
"How many are there, all told?" I asked. "More than a
thousand." "And how are they armed?" "With fish-
bones." "Then," said I, "Our best course is to fight, for
we are armed and they are not, and if we win we shall be
safe."

This was agreed upon and we returned to the ship to
prepare for war. We did not have long to wait. The annual
tribute was due for payment and when, soon after, the
Psittopodians sent messengers to de-
mand it, the old man sent them pack-
ing. The Psittopodians retaliated by
launching a furious attack on Scintharus—for that was the old man's
name. We had expected this and had
twenty-five fully armed men waiting
in ambush for them, with orders to
attack their rear. This they did, falling

on them as soon as they had passed, and cutting them down from behind whilst the rest of us resolutely met them head on and, in the end, put them to flight and chased them back to their dens. One hundred and seventy of them perished whilst we lost our pilot—stabbed in the back with a fishbone and one more besides.

We stayed in our trenches for the rest of that day and all the next night, raising a trophy made from the backbone of a dolphin which we stood on end. The following day the rest of the tribes, with exception of the Tritono-mendetes, having heard the news came out to meet us. Battle was joined near the temple of Poseidon. We charged them with a loud shout which echoed round the inside of the whale as if it were a subterranean cavern. We soon put them to flight, for they did not wear armour, and chased them to the cover of the forest.

Soon after they sent heralds to us to crave for the bodies of their dead

and to sue for peace. But we would not treat with them and put them all to the sword, except for the Tritono-mendetes who, seeing what had happened, rushed to the gills and threw themselves into the sea.

We were now in command of the whole country and lived there from that time on free from enemies, spending our days hunting, growing vines and gathering fruit. We led this life for a year and eight months, but on the fifth day of the month following, at about the second opening of the whale's mouth (for the monster's mouth gaped open once every hour and this was how we told the time) —at about the second opening then, we suddenly heard a great shouting and uproar which sounded like seamen bawling out orders in time with the beat of oars.

With great excitement we crept up into the monster's mouth and standing behind the teeth saw the most amazing sight—giants over three hundred feet high sailing on great Islands just as if they were on board ship! I know it sounds unlikely but there it is: the islands were long but not very high, having a circumference of about eleven miles. Each island had a crew of about twenty-eight giants who sat double-banked, fourteen to each side rowing with great cypress trees, branches, leaves and all, for oars. At the stern, so to speak, standing on a high hill, was the helmsman holding a brass steering oar half a mile long. They had coxswains on board as well who kept the stroke and the islands could be manoeuvred by oars as swiftly as any long boat.

The forest trees growing on the islands served instead of sails, for the wind blowing against them drove the islands along like galleons, following the course steered by the helmsman.

On the "foredeck" stood forty giants, armed for battle,

looking ordinary enough, except for their hair, which was fire and burned clearly so that they did not need helmets.

At first we sighted only two or three islands, but afterwards no less than six hundred appeared and after forming into two lines engaged in battle. They rammed into each other with such force that many immediately capsized or broke up and sank. Others meanwhile closed alongside their adversary and grappled them fast so that it was quite impossible to break free. They used giant squid instead of grappling irons, swinging them aboard the enemy, where, once they got a good hold on the forest trees, they held the island in an unbreakable grip. Then the battle raged furiously, the foredeck soldiers showing great courage by boarding the foe and fighting a merciless hand to hand combat with no quarter given.

The names of the rival leaders were Aeolocentaur and Thalassopot and their dispute was over a herd of dolphins that had been driven off by Thalassopot and that Aeolocentaur said belonged to him. The noise we had first heard was these charges being shouted by the rival factions.

At last Aeolocentaur's fleet was victorious, sinking one hundred and fifty of the enemy's islands for a loss of eighty of his own, and capturing three more with their crews. The rest of Thalassopot's fleet backwatered until it was safe to turn and then fled. Aeolocentaur's ships pursued them a little way but by now it was evening so the victors turned back to make prizes of some more enemy islands that had been disabled and give assistance to some of their own.

To mark their victory they fired a stake in the whale's head and fastened one of the enemy islands to it. That night they lay just off the monster, some moored to him by cables, others anchoring near by. Their anchors were huge, made entirely of glass and very strong.

Next morning, after they had made a sacrifice on the whale's back and buried their dead they sailed away in great triumph singing songs of victory. And that was the end of the battle of the islands.

We now began to grow very tired of life inside the whale and our forced stay there grew more and more irksome. We therefore concentrated all our energies on planning an escape. First of all we thought of boring a tunnel through the monster's right side and making our escape that way. We began digging enthusiastically but after we had made a tunnel half a mile long without result, we gave up. We then decided to set the forest on fire, for we thought that would certainly kill the monster and that once he was dead our escape would be easy. We started at the tail, but it was a whole week before the beast showed any ill effects. On the eighth and ninth days we saw that he was unwell for his jaws drooped open and then closed again quickly. On the tenth and eleventh days a terrible stench showed that putrefaction had set in; on the twelfth day we realized, in the nick of time, that unless we propped up the monster's jaws next time he opened his mouth, we were in danger of being imprisoned inside the dead carcase and should die miserably. This we managed to do, using great baulks of timber. Then we made our ship ready with a store of fresh water and all the provisions we needed. Scintharus was to be our pilot. Next day the whale died.

We hauled the vessel up and making cables fast round the teeth lowered her little by little through one of the gaps and on to the sea.

2

Superstitions and Legends

Sea Superstitions

MICHAEL BROWN

SAILORS, and fishermen in particular, have always been extremely superstitious. This is hardly surprising when one considers the capricious nature of the sea where, even today with our sophisticated weather-forecasting techniques, a sudden storm can blow up quite unexpectedly. In the days before radio and engines, when there could be no long distance communication with another ship or land, and when sail and oar were the only means of propulsion, it was only natural for the sailor to take every precaution to avoid offending the spirits who rule the deep.

One way of propitiating the gods of the sea was to make an annual offering. This custom survives in the ceremony of blessing the sea, which can still be seen once a year in some fishing ports. This Christian ceremony has replaced earlier pagan rites, such as the one which used to be celebrated on the Isle of Lewis. Here an offering was made to a deity called "Shony" on Hallowe'en. The fishermen gathered after dark by the seashore and chose one of their number to make the offering. The "priest" then waded into the sea, bearing a cup of ale and chanting "Shony, I offer you this ale in the hope that you will send us plenty of seaweed to enrich our fishing grounds next year." The ale was then poured into the sea, and everyone adjourned to the nearby church where a lighted candle was standing. The candle was extinguished—a sign that the ritual was over—and the rest of the night was given over to drinking and merriment.

Next to propitiating the sea-gods, the most important thing for the sailor is to know that his boat is free from evil influences. The time to make sure of this is at the launching ceremony. It is clear that the well-known custom of baptizing a ship by breaking a bottle of champagne on her bows goes back a very long way. On the north coast of Brittany new boats were baptized with sea water while the following verse was chanted:

> Bateau n'aie pas peur de cette eau
> Plonge dedans comme un oiseau
> Et te relève aussitôt.
> Mais crains et fuis les rochers
> Car si tu vas les trouver
> Sois sûr dê'tre brisé.

On the north-east coast of Scotland a similar ceremony took place but with whisky substituted for sea-water. In both cases the baptism was followed by drinking and celebration.

Many of these ceremonies clearly had entirely pagan origins, and their purpose was to ward off evil spirits rather than to invoke the aid of the Almighty.

One superstition that does appear to have a Christian origin is the belief that it is unlucky to launch a ship or set sail on a Friday, presumably because this was the day of Christ's crucifixion. In the ballad *The Mermaid* the ship *does* set sail on a Friday and it is this fact, as much as the sighting of the mermaid, that means she is doomed. The mermaid is no more than a harbinger of disaster, not the agent.

I have taken this superstition seriously since a friend of mine tried to launch his yacht on Good Friday. The boat slipped off the trolley going down the slipway, and as she slid into the water, tore a large hole in her bows. She lay in about twelve feet of water and the fire-brigade had to be called to pump her out before she could be hauled up the slip again for repairs. The old sea-dogs round about muttered darkly, with "told-you-so" looks on their faces!

Starting out on a new voyage or fishing trip was a hazardous business at the best of times. Once the seaman had set off for his ship he dared not on any account look back. It was bad luck even to call after him, so if he had forgotten anything someone had to run after him and thrust the object into his hands.

But misfortune could also result from some chance encounter on the way to the boat. In the Shetlands, for example, it was particularly bad luck to meet a hare, a minister of the church or a woman. In such an event the only thing was to turn back and sail next day. The taboo on the hare was because witches were commonly supposed to take this form. The objection to a minister was a throwback to paganism, for the old gods long resented the encroachments of Christianity in the Shetlands, and Thor himself was a mighty fisherman.

Red heads and people with flat feet were also to be avoided, but if one did chance to meet them bad luck could be averted by speaking to them first. For fishermen it was an ill omen to see a dog near his tackle. Cats on the other hand were considered lucky, especially black cats. Some fishermen's wives believed a black cat would bring their husbands back from the sea and it was known for

domestic cats to mysteriously disappear from inland towns and turn up in fishing villages!

If the sailor was to have any chance at all of making a safe return certain other taboos had to be observed. In Iceland small boys had to be prevented from throwing stones into the sea, for this would cause heavy breakers and perhaps storms; it was also extremely unlucky to throw a stone over a vessel putting to sea, for this meant it would never return. Again the ringing note made by the rim of a glass would mean a shipwreck unless it was quickly stopped by putting a finger on the rim.

Once afloat the seaman's problems were by no means over. It was an ill omen to see certain birds at sea. French channel fishermen feared the cormorant, while the men of Dover and Folkestone were afraid of the curlew. Sea-gulls were widely believed to embody the spirits of drowned sailors, for this reason they must never be killed, but should be fed and treated kindly. Swallows seen at sea are a good omen whilst wild geese flying north off the coast of Scotland are held to bring good weather:

> "Wild geese, wild geese, gangin t' the sea
> Good weather it will be."

If porpoises are seen swimming round a vessel it is a very good sign, but it would be very unlucky to try and catch one.

In the days before steam, sailors were sometimes forced to whistle for a wind. This was a dangerous thing to do, for it meant summoning aid from unseen powers and one might easily get more than one bargained for. The wise thing to do was to stick a knife in the mast (iron commands respect from the unseen) and whistle softly. I used to try this for myself when I started sailing and when, as so often happened, it didn't work, I consoled myself with the thought that I had whistled the wrong tune or made some other mistake in the ritual that had offended the wind spirit.

Among seamen Finns are reputed to have power over the wind, a gift that had greater significance in the days of sail than now. The tradition is an old one and Finnish wizards were supposed to be able to tie the wind up in a bag with three knots. As each knot was untied the wind grew stronger.

Frazer writes in *The Golden Bough*: "It is said, too, that

sailors, beating up against the wind in the Gulf of Finland, sometimes see a strange sail heave in sight astern and overhaul them hand over hand. On she comes with a cloud canvas—all her studding sails out—right in the teeth of the wind, forging her way through the foaming billows, dashing back the spray in sheets from her cut-water, every sail swollen to bursting, every rope strained to cracking. Then the sailors know she hails from Finland."

There were very often Finnish sailors on board the sailing ships of the nineteenth and early twentieth centuries and they were treated with the utmost circumspection for fear they should call up contrary winds. In *Two Years Before the Mast* Richard Dana quotes the following story: "John said that he himself had been in a ship where they had a head wind for a fortnight, and the captain found out at last that one of the men, with whom he had had some hard words a short time before, was a Finn, and immediately told him if he didn't stop the head wind he would shut him down in the fore-peak. The Finn would not give in, and the captain shut him down in the fore-peak and would not give him anything to eat. The Finn held out for a day and a half, when he could not stand it any longer and did something or other which brought the wind round, and they let him up."

French sailors had their own way of raising a breeze: by flogging the wretched cabin boy with his back turned in the direction from which the wind was required.

Probably the most awe-inspiring omen that the sailor is likely to encounter at sea is St. Elmo's fire. This eerie, glowing flame that sometimes appears on the masts and yard arms of ships is caused by electrical discharges in a storm. The phenomenon is occasionally accompanied by a cracking noise like the sound of dry twigs burning.

St. Elmo (Erasmus) is the patron saint of Mediterranean seamen and he is said to have died at sea during a storm. Before he died he promised to return and show himself to the crew in some form as a sign that they would survive the storm. Soon afterwards a strange light appeared at the masthead and the sailors were saved. In Spain and Portugal the fire was known as Corpus Santo ("body of the saint"—referring of course to St. Elmo) which was corrupted by English sailors into Corposant. A very good description is to be found in *Two Years Before the Mast*. Dana and an English sailor have just come down on deck after furling a sail: "When we got down, we found all hands looking aloft, and there, directly over where we had been standing, upon the maintopgallant mast-head, was a ball of light, which the sailors call a corposant, and which the mate had called out to us to look at. They were all watching it carefully, for sailors have a notion that if the corposant rises in the rigging it is a sign of fair weather, but if it comes lower down there will be a storm. Unfortunately, as an omen, it came down, and showed itself on the topgallant yard-arm. We were off the yard in good season, for it is held a fatal sign to have the pale light of the corposant thrown upon one's face. As it was, the English lad did not feel comfortable at having had it so near him, and directly over his head. In a few minutes it disappeared, and showed itself again on the foretopgallant yard; and, after playing about for some time, disappeared once more."

If the corposant shone round a seaman's head like a halo he was doomed.

Seagulls are sometimes the harbingers of death. When three of them are seen flying together overhead it is a bad omen either for the person who sees them or for someone close to him. A lone gull flying in a straight line over the sea is said to be following the drift of a corpse on the sea bed. The seagull is the soul of the dead man and is tied to the unburied body which cannot find rest. John Masefield tells the story of two Norwegians bound homeward from San Francisco who quarrelled as to which of them was the best dancer. One killed the other and threw him overboard. From then on at dawn each day a white gull flew screaming after the ship. It was the spirit of the dead Norwegian and when the ship reached Norway the murderer gave himself up.

If a gull should fly against the window of a house it is warning of danger to some relative at sea.

Scandinavian fishermen believed that before a man died the oars of his boat were turned round by invisible hands. On the coast of Fife in Scotland it was believed that the Kelpie—a black horse with staring eyes—would appear from the sea to warn the womenfolk of a disaster at sea.

Death has often been linked with the rising or ebbing of the tide, for example, in *David Copperfield* where Dickens writes of the death of Barkis: "And it being low water, he went out with the tide."

In Brittany it was believed that the dead were transported to the Isles of the Blessed—somewhere to the West. The spirits of the departed gathered at the Bay of Souls near the Point du Raz until the soul ship arrived. In Cornwall, too, there are traditions of phantom ships, but in this case they come to collect the souls of the damned.

Seamen are naturally very superstitious about drowning. In the old days sailors never learned to swim, believing that if they fell overboard it was useless to fight the sea. So strong was this superstition that in some cases they would even refuse to try and rescue a drowning man. The very word "drown" was never to be spoken at sea, for fear of the consequences.

It was thought that the drowned could be heard wailing their names at the height of a bad storm. Robert Hunt, in *Popular Romances of the West* says: "The fishermen dread to walk at night near those parts of the shore where there may have been wrecks. The souls of drowned sailors appear to haunt those spots and 'the calling of the dead' has frequently been heard. I have been told that, under certain circumstances, especially before the coming of storms, or at certain seasons, but always at night these callings are common. Many a fisherman has declared he has heard the voices of dead sailors hailing their own names."

A different kind of sound is heard at midnight in a churchyard at Land's End in Cornwall. It is the ghostly ringing of a ship's bell from the grave of a sea captain whose ship sank just as he was striking eight bells. Sailors believe that the ship's bell is the soul of the ship and that it will always ring when a ship is wrecked.

These are just a few of the superstitions connected with the sea. The origins of many of them are very ancient indeed, going far back into pagan times. Nowadays many of the superstitions have been forgotten but it is amazing how many still keep their hold.

The Albatross

R. P. LISTER

It was commonly believed amongst seamen that if one of them was drowned at sea his spirit would pass into the body of a sea-gull. It is this ancient superstition that lies behind the Rime of the Ancient Mariner. *In Coleridge's poem the mariner brings misfortune upon his head by shooting an Albatross and ever since the idea that it is bad luck to kill this splendid bird has been widespread. And yet, I do not believe that there was any particular taboo against killing an Albatross, for whenever this superstition is cited the only source that is ever mentioned is the* Rime of the Ancient Mariner. *The fact that the superstition is so firmly entrenched seems more a tribute to Coleridge's imaginative power, than a proof of its truth. Indeed it would be odd if such a taboo were associated with such a rare bird. The Albatross is after all normally only found in the Southern Oceans in what seamen call the Roaring Forties (between 40° and 50° south). On the contrary the sailors on board the big square riggers at the turn of the last century made horrible sport by towing a baited hook and line over the stern. The Albatross would take the bait, be hooked by the beak, hauled on board and killed. There is no evidence to suggest that these mariners met a terrible fate as a result. I don't advise killing a sea-gull, however.*

I sailed below the Southern Cross
   (so ran the seaman's song);
A pestilential albatross
   Followed us all day long.

The creature's aspect was so grim,
   And it oppressed me so,
I raised . . . then, on a sudden whim,
   I lowered my crossbow.

The weather grew exceeding thick;
   The sullen tempest roared.
A dozen of the crew fell sick,
   The rest fell overboard.

The skies were so devoid of light
   We could not see to pray.
The donkeyman went mad by night,
   The second mate by day.

We set the live men swabbing decks,
   The dead man manned the pumps.
The cabin steward changed his sex;
   The captain had the mumps.

The cargo shifted in the hold,
   The galley boiler burst.
My hair turned white, my blood ran cold—
   I knew we were accurst.

I helped the purser dig his grave
   On the deserted poop;
I leaped into the foaming wave
   And swam to Guadeloupe.

And there (he said) I nibbled moss
   Beside the stagnant lake . . .
I should have shot the albatross,
   That was my big mistake.

Boat Language

JON ARNASON

SOMETIMES one may hear a certain kind of cracking in boats that are in the boat-stand in calm weather. This cracking is the language of the boats, which it is not for everyone to understand. But one man, on a time, understood the boat language. He came to the sea shore when two boats were standing close together, and was witness that they thus talked:

1st Boat: "Long have we been together, but tomorrow must we part company."

2nd Boat: "Nay! that shall never be; we must not part. Thirty years now have we been neighbours, and grown old; and if one is wrecked, we shall both go under."

1st Boat: "Natheless, that will not be: Good weather to-night, but other weather tomorrow, and none will row out but thy master; but I shall be left behind, and also the other boats. But thou wilt go, never to return. Never more shall we stand here together."

2nd Boat: "That never shall be, nor will I let myself be launched."

1st Boat: "Bound thou wilt be to go down to the sea. This is the last of nights that we shall be together."

2nd Boat: "Never will I let myself be launched, without thou goest down with me into the sea."

1st Boat: "It is not to be avoided."

2nd Boat: "Nay! without the devil himself come too."

After this the boats spoke in so low a voice, that the listener was unable to make out their secret mutterings.

Next morning the weather was very suspicious, and deemed not fit to row out, except by one boat-master and his crew. Down to the sea they went, as did many who would not out-row.

"Now," said the boat-master, as wont he was, "your skin-clothes on, in Jesus' name." And the crew clothed them in their skin-clothes.

"Let us launch the boat, in Jesus' name," quoth the boat-master, as wont he was.

So they all fell to launching, but the boat was not to be moved.

The boat-master prayed the other boat-men, who stood by, to aid them; but neither was this of any avail. Now every one of the standers by had lent his aid to launch the boat, and the master said, as before, "Now, let us launch in Jesus' name"; but, in spite of all the hands at work, not an inch moved the boat.

Then cried the master loud, and said: "Hallo, there! In the name of the devil, forth with it!"

No sooner had the words been spoken than forth shot the boat into the sea, and nigh had flung itself out of the grasp of the men who launched it.

Now out, and away, went this boat with its crew; but nought has ever been seen of the boat since, nor aught been heard of its crew.

The Cormorants of Udröst

P. C. ASBJÖRNSEN

Bright, 'mid the skerries of the Western sea
An island rides upon the wave. Yet none
May know its beauty; for if mortal ship
By chance should drift too near th' enchanted shore
A curtain of dark mist enshrouds the isle.
No eye can see its brightness, and no foot
May leave its print upon the golden fields.
'Tis but in fancy he who dwells ashore
May picture, in the longings of his dreams,
This fairy jewel of the Western sea.

WHEN the fishermen in the north of Norway come to land, they often find straw stuck between the rudder and the stern-post, or grain in the stomach of the fish. It is then said, that they have sailed over Udröst or some of the other fairy-lands, about which so many legends are told in the north. These fairy-lands are only seen by very pious people or by those who are gifted with second sight, when in danger of their lives at sea, and they appear where at other times no land is to be found. The supernatural people who live here have farms and keep cattle, fish and own ships, like other folks, but here the sun shines on greener pastures and richer corn fields than elsewhere in the north; and fortunate, indeed, is he who landed on or even has seen one of these sunny isles;—"he is a made man," say the people in the north.

87

An old ballad, in the style of Peder Dass, gives a full description of an island off Traenen in Helgeland, called Sandflaesen, with rich fisheries and abounding with game of all sorts. In the middle of the Vestford a large flat land with rich corn fields also appears, but it only rises high enough above the surface of the water to leave the ears of the corn dry; and outside Röst, off the southern point of the Lofoten islands, a similar fairy land with green hills and golden barley fields is spoken of, which is called Udröst. The farmer on Udröst owns his fishing-smack just like any other farmer in the north; sometimes the fishermen see it under full sails, and steering right down upon them, but just as they expect to be run down, it disappears.

On Vaerö, not far from Röst, lived once a poor fisherman, whose name was Isaac. All he possessed was a boat and a couple of goats, which his wife managed to keep alive on fish-offal, and the few stray wisps of grass to be found on the neighbouring cliffs; but he had a whole cottage full of hungry children. But still Isaac seemed always to be satisfied with the lot Providence had ordained for him. His only complaint was, that he could never be left in peace by his neighbour, who was a well-to-do man, and fancied that he ought to have everything better than such riff-raff as Isaac. He wanted, therefore, to get rid of Isaac that he might have the harbour in front of Isaac's cottage.

One day when Isaac was out fishing a good many miles out at sea a thick, dark fog came upon him, and before long a tremendous gale broke loose, and raged with such a fury that he had to throw all the fish overboard to lighten the boat and save his life.

Still it was no easy task to keep the boat afloat; but he knew well how to handle his little craft, and how to steer her among the heavy seas, which every moment threatened to swamp her. When he had been sailing at this rate for five or six hours, he thought he ought soon to sight land somewhere. But hour after hour passed and the storm and thick fog got worse and worse. Then it dawned upon him that he must be steering right out to sea, or that the wind had shifted; and at last he felt sure that he must have guessed right, for he sailed and sailed, but saw no sign of land. All of a sudden he heard a terrible scream ahead, and he thought it must be the bogie singing his dirge. He prayed for his wife and children, for he knew now that his last hour had come; but while he sat and prayed he caught sight of something black, and as he came nearer he saw it was only three cormorants sitting on a piece of drift-wood; the next moment he had sailed past them. So the time wore on, and he began to feel so thirsty and so hungry and so tired that he did not for the life of him know what to do. He sat half asleep with the tiller in his hand, when all at once the boat grated against the beach and ran aground. Isaac was not long in getting his eyes open. The sun was breaking through the fog and shone upon a splendid country; the hills and the cliffs were green right to the top, with meadows and cornfields on the slopes, and he thought he felt a scent of flowers and grass which he never had felt before.

"The Lord be praised," said Isaac to himself. "I am safe now; this must be Udröst." Straight before him was a field of barley with ears so large and full that he had never seen their like, and through this field a narrow path led up to a green turf-roofed hut at the other end of the cornfield. On the roof of the hut was a white goat with gilt horns, grazing; its udder was as large as the largest cow's. Outside the hut sat a little old man on a wooden stool, smoking a cutty-pipe. He was dressed in blue, and had a full long beard which reached down to his waist.

"Welcome to Udröst, Isaac!" said the old man.

"Thank you!" answered Isaac. "You know me then?"

"Perhaps I do." said the man. "You want to stop here tonight, I suppose?"

"Well, if I might I should like nothing better," said Isaac.

"It's rather awkward with those sons of mine," said the old man; "they don't like the smell of Christians. Have you not met them?"

"No, I have met nothing but three cormorants, which were sitting on a bit of drift-wood screeching."

"Yes, those were my sons, those were," said the old old man, as he knocked the ashes out of his pipe. "You had better go inside meantime. I suppose you are both hungry and thirsty?"

"Thanks for your offer, my friend," said Isaac. But when the man opened the door, he found it was such a fine and grand place inside, that he was quite taken aback. He had never seen anything like it before. The table was covered with the most splendid dishes, sea perch and sour cream, venison and cod-liver stew with treacle and cheese, heaps of cakes, brandy, beer and mead, in fact, everything that was good. Isaac ate and drank as much as he was able, but still his plate never became empty, and although he drank a good deal, his glass was always full. The old man did not eat much, and he did not speak much either; but just then they heard a scream and a great noise outside. Isaac felt a little queer when the old man's sons came in, but the old man must have been telling them to behave themselves, for they were kind and pleasant enough. They said he must follow their custom and sit down and drink with them, for Isaac was going to leave the table; he had been doing very well, he said. But he did as they wished, and they drank glass after glass, and now and then they took a pull at the beer and the mead. They became good friends and got on very well together. Isaac must go fishing a trip or two with them, they said, so that he could have something to take home with him when he went away.

The first trip they made was in a terrible gale. One of the sons was steering, the other held the sheet, and the third son was 'midships, while Isaac bailed out the water with a big scoop until the perspiration ran down his back in big drops. They sailed as if they were stark mad; they never took in a reef in the sail, and when the seas filled the boat, they sailed her up on the back of a wave till she stood nearly on end, the water rushing out over her stern as out of a spout. Shortly the storm abated, and they commenced to fish. The fish were so thickly packed, that the lead could not reach the bottom. The young men from Udröst hauled in one fish after another, and Isaac had also plenty of bites, but he had brought his own fishing tackle with him, and every time he got a fish as far as the gunwale it got off; he did not catch as much as the tail of one. When the boat was full, they sailed home to Udröst. The sons cut up the fish, and cleaned them and hung them up across some poles to dry, but Isaac could only complain of his bad fortune to the old man, who promised him better luck next time and gave him a couple of fish-hooks. The next time they went fishing Isaac caught as much fish as the others, and when they came ashore and hung up their fish, he had three long poles full for his share.

Isaac soon began to feel homesick, and when he was leaving the old man made him a present of a new eight-oared boat, filled with bags of flour, canvas, and other useful things, for which Isaac tendered his best thanks. The old man told him to come back again by the time the fishing smacks were about to start for their yearly trips to Bergen, where he was going himself with a cargo, and Isaac could go with him and sell his fish. Yes, Isaac would be pleased to do that, and asked what course he was to steer when he sailed for Udröst again.

"Straight after the cormorants, when they fly to sea," said the man. "That's your right course, and a safe journey to you!"

But when Isaac had shoved off from the shore and turned round to give his friends a farewell look, Udröst was not to be seen any more; he saw only the open sea far and near.

When the time came for the smacks to start, Isaac arrived at Udröst. But such a smack as the old man had Isaac had never seen before; it was two cables long, and the mate, who stood forward on the look out, could not shout loud enough to make himself heard by the man at the helm. They had therefore to station another man amidships close to the mast, and he had to sing out to the man at the helm, and even then he had to shout as loud as as he could to make himself heard. Isaac's share of the cargo was stowed forward in the smack; he took the fish down off the poles himself, but he could not make out how it came to pass, for as soon as he took the fish off the poles, they were full of new fish again, and when they sailed, there was just as much fish as when he came. When he came to Bergen, he sold his fish, and got so much money, that he bought a new smack, with cargo and everything that was wanted for a good outfit, just as the old man had advised him to do. Late in the evening before he was going to sail, the old man came on board to him and asked him not to forget those whom his neighbour had left behind him, when he was lost at sea, and then he prophesied Isaac good luck with his smack.

"Everything on board is sound and good, and you may be sure that all aloft will stand," said he, meaning that there would always be one on board whom nobody could see, who at a pinch would put his back to the mast and steady it. Isaac was always very successful after that time. He knew well where his good luck came from, and he never forgot to provide well for the man who kept watch on board when the smack was laid up for winter, and every Christmas Eve there was such a glare of light from the smack that it could be seen afar off, and then you could hear the sound of fiddles and music, and laughter, and merriment, while there was dancing going on in the cabin of the smack.

The Fisherman and the Draug

JONAS LIE

The Draug is a sea-spirit who haunts the waters of northern Norway sailing in a strange halfboat. Fishermen say he can assume any shape at will but he is most often seen in the guise of a sailor man—without a head! In some parts of Norway, however, they maintain that he has a tin-plate on his neck with burning coals for eyes.

Sometimes at sea the fishermen hear a dreadful wailing cry that sounds like "so cold"—then they hasten to the shore, for the Draug's lament is warning of a storm.

Ashore the Draug is usually to be found near the boats or in the boatshed. If the fisherman finds a kind of foam in his boat it is the Draug's vomit and a sign of death.

NAUTICAL TERMS: Sexaering: *a rowing boat with three pairs of oars.* Fëmboring: *a large fishing boat with five pairs of oars.* Take in a clew: *to reef. In the old days sails were reefed (i.e. a smaller area exposed to the wind) by bunching up the bottom of the sail and tying a horizontal row of short pieces of line, called reef points, sewn on both sides of the sail. At the end of each line of reef points was a clew ring—a brass ring to which was attached the mainsheets, the rope that controls the amount the sail is let in or out. Each time the sail was reefed one clew ring was rendered useless and the mainsheets had to be moved up to the next ring above. Hence to "take in four clews" meant to take in three rows of reef points. This would reduce the sail area by half or two-thirds.*

O N Kvalholm, dwelt a poor fisherman, Elias by name, with his wife Karen, who had been in service at the parson's over at Alstad. They built them a hut here, and he used to go out fishing by the day about the Lofotens.

95

There could be very little doubt that the lonely Kval-holm was haunted. Whenever her husband was away, Karen heard all manner of uncanny shrieks and noises, which could mean no good. One day, when she was up on the hillside, mowing grass to serve as winter fodder for their sheep, she heard, quite plainly, a chattering on the strand beneath the hill, but look over she durst not.

They had a child every year, but that was no burden, for they were both thrifty, hard-working folks. When seven years had gone by, there were six children in the house; but that same autumn Elias had scraped together so much that he thought he might now venture to buy a *Sexæring*, and henceforward go fishing in his own boat.

One day, as he was walking along with a harpoon in his hand, and thinking the matter over, he unexpectedly came upon a monstrous seal, which lay sunning itself right behind a rock on the strand, and was as much surprised to see the man as the man was to see the seal. But Elias was not slack; from the top of the rock on which he stood, he hurled the long heavy harpoon right into the monster's back, just below the neck.

The seal immediately rose up on its tail right into the air as high as a boat's mast, and looked so evilly and viciously at him with its bloodshot eyes, at the same time showing its grinning teeth, that Elias thought he should have died on the spot for sheer fright. Then it plunged into the sea, and lashed the water into bloody foam behind it. Elias didn't stop to see more, but that same evening there drifted into the boat place where his house stood, a harpoon, with its iron spiked head snapped off.

Elias thought no more about it, but in the course of the autumn he bought his *Sexæring*, for which he had been building a little boat-shed the whole summer.

One night as he lay awake, thinking of his new *Sexæ-ring*, it occurred to him that his boat would balance better perhaps, if he stuck an extra log of wood on each side of it. He was so absurdly fond of the boat that he used to light a lantern and go down to have a look at it.

Now as he stood looking at it there by the light of the lantern, he suddenly caught a glimpse in the corner opposite, on a coil of nets, of a face which exactly resembled the seal's. For an instant it grinned savagely at him and the light, its mouth all the time growing larger; and then a big man whisked out of the door, not so quickly, however, but Elias could catch a glimpse, by the light of the lantern, of a long iron hooked spike sticking out of his back. And now he began to put one and two together. Still he was less anxious about his life than about his boat; so he there and then sat him down in it with the lantern, and kept watch. When his wife came in the morning, she found him sleeping there, with the burnt-out lantern by his side.

One morning in January, while he was out fishing in his boat with two other men, he heard, in the dark, a voice from a skerry at the very entrance of the creek. It laughed scornfully, and said, "When it *comes to a Femböring*, Elias, look to thyself!"

But there was many a long year yet before it *did* come to that; but one autumn, when his son Bernt was sixteen, Elias knew he could manage it, so he took his whole family with him in his boat to the port of Ranen, to exchange his *Sexæring* for a *Femböring*. The only person left at home was a little Finn girl, whom they had taken into service some few years before, and who had only lately been confirmed.

Now there was a boat, a little *Femböring*, for four men

and a boy, that Elias just then had his eye upon—a boat which the best boat-builder in the place had finished and tarred over that very autumn. Elias had a very good notion of what a boat should be, and it seemed to him that he had never seen a *Femböring* so well built *below* the water-line. *Above* the water-line, indeed, it looked only middling, so that, to one of less experience than himself, the boat would have seemed rather a heavy goer than otherwise, and anything but a smart craft.

Now the boat-master knew all this just as well as Elias. He said he thought it would be the swiftest sailer in Ranen, but that Elias should have it cheap, all the same, if only he would promise one thing, and that was, to make no alteration whatever in the boat, nay, not so much as adding a fresh coat of tar. Only when Elias had expressly given his word upon it did he get the boat.

But the devil had taught the boat-master how to build his boats cunningly *below* the water-line—*above* the water-line he had had to use his native wits, and they were scant enough—must surely have been there beforehand, and bidden him both sell it cheaply, so that Elias might get it, and stipulate besides that the boat should not be looked at too closely. In this way it escaped the usual tarring fore and aft.

Elias now thought about sailing home, but went first into town, provided himself and family with provisions against Christmas, and indulged in a little nip of brandy besides. Glad as he was over the day's bargain, he, and his wife too, took an extra drop in their e'en, and their son Bernt had a taste of it too.

After that they sailed off homewards in their new boat. There was no other ballast in the boat but himself, his old woman, the children, and the Christmas provisions. His son Bernt sat by the main-sheet; his wife, helped by her next eldest son, held the sail-ropes; Elias himself sat at the rudder, while the two younger brothers of twelve and fourteen were to take it in turns to bail out.

They had eight miles of sea to sail over, and when they got into the open, it was plain that the boat would be tested pretty stiffly on its first voyage. A gale was gradually blowing up, and crests of foam began to break upon the heavy sea.

And now Elias saw what sort of boat he really had. She skipped over the waves like a sea-mew; not so much as a splash came into the boat, and he therefore calculated that he would have no need to take in all his clews against the wind, which an ordinary *Femböring* would have been forced to do in such weather.

Out on the sea, not very far away from him, he saw another *Femböring*, with a full crew, and four clews in the sail, just like his own. It lay on the same course, and he thought it rather odd that he had not noticed it before. It made as if it would race him, and when Elias perceived that, he could not for the life of him help letting out a clew again.

And now he went racing along like a dart, past capes and islands and rocks, till it seemed to Elias as if he had never had such a splendid sail before. Now, too, the boat showed itself what it really was, the best boat in Ranen.

The weather, meantime, had become worse, and they got a couple of dangerous seas right upon them. They broke in over the mainsheet in the forepart of the boat where Bernt sat, and sailed out again to leeward near the stern.

Since the gloom had deepened, the other boat had kept

almost alongside, and they were now so close they could easily have pitched the baling-can from one to the other.

So they raced on, side by side, in constantly stiffer seas, till night-fall, and beyond it. The fourth clew ought now to have been taken in again, but Elias didn't want to give in, and thought he might bide a bit till they took it in in the other boat also, which they needs *must* do soon. Ever and anon the brandy-flask was brought out and passed round, for they had now both cold and wet to hold out against.

The sea-fire, which played on the dark billows near Elias's own boat, shone with an odd vividness in the foam round the other boat, just as if a fire-shovel was ploughing up and turning over the water. In the bright phosphorescence he could plainly make out the rope-ends on board her. He could also see distinctly the folks on board, with their sou'westers on their heads; but as their larboard side lay nearest, of course they all had their backs towards him, and were well-nigh hidden by the high heeling hull.

Suddenly a tremendous roller burst upon them. Elias had long caught a glimpse of its white crest through the darkness, right over the prow where Bernt sat. It filled the whole boat for a moment, the planks shook and trembled beneath the weight of it, and then, as the boat, which had lain half on her beam-ends, righted herself and sped on again, it streamed off behind to leeward.

While it was still upon him, he fancied he heard a hideous yell from the other boat; but when it was over, his wife, who sat by the shrouds, said, with a voice which pierced his very soul: "Good God, Elias! the sea has carried off Martha and Nils!"—their two youngest children, the first nine, the second seven years old, who had been sitting in the hold near Bernt. Elias merely answered: "Don't let go the lines, Karen, or you'll lose yet more!"

They had now to take in the fourth clew, and, when this was done, Elias found that it would be well to take in the fifth and last clew too, for the gale was ever on the increase; but, on the other hand, in order to keep the boat free of the constantly heavier seas, he dare not lessen the sail a bit more than he was absolutely obliged to do; but they found that the scrap of sail they could carry gradually grew less and less. The sea seethed so that it drove right into their faces, and Bernt and his next eldest brother Anthony, who had hitherto helped his mother with the sail-lines, had, at last, to hold in the yards, an expedient one only resorts to when the boat cannot bear even the last clew—here the fifth.

The companion boat, which had disappeared in the meantime, now suddenly ducked up alongside again, with precisely the same amount of sail as Elias's boat; but he now began to feel that he didn't quite like the look of the crew on board there. The two who stood and held in the yards (he caught a glimpse of their pale faces beneath their sou'westers) seemed to him, by the odd light of the shining foam, more like corpses than men, nor did they speak a single word.

A little way off to larboard he again caught sight of the high white back of a fresh roller coming through the dark, and he got ready betimes to receive it. The boat was laid to with its prow turned aslant towards the on-rushing wave, while the sail was made as large as possible, so as to get up speed enough to cleave the heavy sea and sail out of it again. In rushed the roller with a roar like a foss; again, for an instant, they lay on their beam ends; but, when it was over, the wife no longer sat by the sail ropes, nor did Anthony stand there any longer holding the yards —they had both gone overboard.

This time also Elias fancied he heard the same hideous yell in the air; but in the midst of it he plainly heard his wife anxiously calling him by name. All that he said when he grasped the fact that she was washed overboard, was, "In Jesus' Name!" His first and dearest wish was to follow after her, but he felt at the same time that it became him to save the rest of the freight he had on board, that is to say, Bernt and his other two sons, one twelve, the other fourteen years old, who had been baling out for a time, but had afterwards taken their places in the stern behind him.

Bernt had now to look to the yards all alone, and the other two helped as best they could. The rudder Elias durst not let slip, and he held it fast with a hand of iron, which continuous exertion had long since made insensible to feeling.

A moment afterwards the comrade boat ducked up again: it had vanished for an instant as before. Now, too, he saw more of the heavy man who sat in the stern there in the same place as himself. Out of his back, just below his sou'wester (as he turned round it showed quite plainly), projected an iron spike six inches long, which Elias had no difficulty in recognizing again. And now, as he calmly thought it all over, he was quite clear about two things: one was the Draug itself which was steering its half-boat close beside him and leading him to destruction; the other was that it was written in heaven that he was to sail his last course that night. For he who sees the Draug on the sea is a doomed man. He said nothing to the others, lest they should lose heart, but in secret he commended his soul to God.

During the last hour or so he had been forced out of his proper course by the storm; the air also had become dense with snow; and Elias knew that he must wait till dawn before land could be sighted. Meanwhile he sailed along much as before. Now and then the boys in the stern complained that they were freezing; but, in the plight they were now in, that couldn't be helped, and, besides, Elias had something else to think about. A terrible longing for vengeance had come over him, and, but for the necessity of saving the lives of his three lads, he would have tried by a sudden turn to sink the accursed boat which kept alongside of him the whole time as if to mock him; he now understood its evil errand only too well, and he felt that he would gladly have given his life for one good grip of the being who had so mercilessly torn from him his dearest in this world and would fain have still more.

At three or four o'clock in the morning they saw coming upon them through the darkness a breaker of such a height that at first Elias thought they must be quite close ashore near the surf swell. Nevertheless, he soon recognized it for what it really was—a huge billow. Then it seemed to him as if there was a laugh over in the other boat, and something said, "There goes thy boat, Elias!" He, foreseeing the calamity, now cried aloud: "In Jesus' Name!" and then bade his sons hold on with all their might to the withy-bands by the rowlocks when the boat went under, and not let go till it was above water again. He made the elder of them go forward to Bernt; and himself held the youngest close by his side, stroked him once or twice furtively down the cheeks, and made sure that he had a good grip. The boat, literally buried beneath the foaming roller, was lifted gradually up by the bows and then went under. When it rose again out of the water, with the keel in the air, Elias, Bernt, and the twelve-year-old Martin lay alongside, holding on by the withy-bands; but the third of the brothers was gone.

They had now first of all to get the shrouds on one side cut through, so that the mast might come to the surface alongside instead of disturbing the balance of the boat below; and then they must climb up on the swaying bottom of the boat and stave in the key-holes, to let out the air which kept the boat too high in the water, and so ease her. After great exertions they succeeded, and Elias, who had got up on top first, now helped the other two after him.

There they sat through the long dark winter night, clinging convulsively on by their hands and knees to the boat's bottom, which was drenched by the billows again and again.

After the lapse of a couple of hours died Martin, whom his father had held up the whole time as far as he was able, of sheer exhaustion, and glided down into the sea. They had tried to cry for help several times, but gave it up at last as a bad job.

Whilst they two thus sat alone on the bottom of the boat, Elias said to Bernt he must now needs believe that he too was about to die, but that he had a strong hope that Bernt, at any rate, would be saved, if he only held out like a man. Then he told him all about the Draug, and how it had now revenged itself upon him, and certainly would not forbear till it was "quits with him".

It was towards nine o'clock in the morning when grey dawn began to appear. Then Elias gave to Bernt, who sat alongside him, his silver watch with the brass chain, which he had snapped in two in order to drag it from beneath his closely buttoned jacket. He held on for a little time longer, but, as it got lighter, Bernt saw that his father's face was deadly pale, his hair too had parted here and there, as often happens when death is at hand, and his skin was chafed off his hands from holding on to the keel. The son understood now that his father was nearly at the last gasp, and tried, so far as the pitching and tossing would allow it, to hold him up; but when Elias marked it, he said, "Nay, look to thyself, Bernt, and hold on fast. I go to mother—in Jesus' Name!" and with that he cast himself down headlong from the top of the boat.

Every one who has sat on the keel of a boat long enough knows that when the sea has got its own it grows much calmer, though not immediately. Bernt now found it easier to hold on, and still more of hope came to him with the brightening day. The storm abated, and, when it got quite light, it seemed to him that he knew where he was, and that it was outside his own homestead, Kvalholm, that he lay driving.

He now began again to cry for help, but his chief hope was in a current which he knew bore landwards at a place where a headland broke in upon the surge, and there the water was calmer. And he did, in fact, drive closer and closer in, and came at last so near to one of the rocks that the mast, which was floating by the side of the boat all the time, surged up and down in the swell against the sloping cliff. Stiff as he now was in all his limbs from sitting and holding on, he nevertheless succeeded, after a great effort, in clambering up the cliff, where he hauled the mast ashore, and made the *Femböring* fast.

The Finn girl, who was alone in the house, had been thinking, for the last two hours, that she had heard cries for help from time to time, and as they kept on she mounted the hill to see what it was. There she saw Bernt up on the cliff, and the overturned *Femböring* bobbing up and down against it. She immediately dashed down to the boat-place, got out the old rowing-boat, and rowed along the shore and round the island right out to him.

Bernt lay sick under her care the whole winter through, and didn't go a fishing all that year. Ever after this, too, it seemed to folks as if the lad were a little bit daft.

On the open sea he never would go again, for he had got the sea-scare. He wedded the Finn girl, and moved over to Malang, where he got him a clearing in the forest, and he lives there now, and is doing well, they say.

Finn Blood

JONAS LIE

True Finns belong to a mysterious race called the Suomi who are found not only in modern Finland but also on the Baltic coast of Russia. They are closely related to the Lapps, Estonians and other peoples of north-east Europe and Scandinavia.

Because of their reputation for skill in magic, Finns hold a unique place in the folklore of the sea. Sailormen regarded them with awe because they were believed to have power to control the wind, whilst it was also widely held that they could change themselves into seals and other animals at will. In the Orkney and Shetland Islands the term "Finn" was commonly used to describe a human in animal form without any suggestion that he or she belonged the Finnish race. The Great Silkie of Sule Skerrie is a "Finn" in this sense.

IN Svartfjord, north of Senje, dwelt a lad called Eilert. His neighbours were seafaring Finns, and among their children was a pale little girl, remarkable for her long black hair and her large eyes. They dwelt behind the crag on the other side of the promontory, and fished for a livelihood, as also did Eilert's parents; wherefore there was no particular goodwill between the families, for the nearest fishing ground was but a small one, and each would have liked to have rowed there alone.

Nevertheless, though his parents didn't like it at all, and even forbade it, Eilert used to sneak regularly down to the Finns. There they had always strange tales to tell, and he heard wondrous things about the recesses of the mountains, where the original home of the Finns was, and where, in olden time dwelt the Finn Kings, who were masters among the magicians. There, too, he heard tell of all that was beneath the sea, where the Mermen and the Draugs hold sway. The latter are gloomy evil powers, and many a time his blood stood still in his veins as he sat and listened. They told him that the Draug usually showed himself on the strand in the moonlight on those spots which were covered with sea-wrack; that he had a bunch of seaweed instead of a head, but shaped so peculiarly that whoever came across him couldn't help gazing into his pale and horrible face. They themselves had seen him many a time, and once they had driven him, thwart by thwart, out of the boat where he had sat one morning, and turned the oars upside down. When Eilert hastened homewards in the darkness round the headland, along the strand, over heaps of seaweed, he dare scarcely look around him, and many a time the sweat absolutely streamed from his forehead.

In proportion as hostility increased among the old people, they had a good deal of fault to find with one another, and Eilert heard no end of evil things spoken about the Finns at home. Now it was this, and now it was that. They didn't even row like honest folk, for, after the Finnish fashion, they took high and swift strokes, as if they were womenkind, and they all talked together, and made a noise while they rowed, instead of being "silent in the boat". But what impressed Eilert most of all was the fact that, in the Finnwoman's family, they practised sorcery and idolatry, or so folks said. He also heard tell of something beyond all question, and that was the shame of having Finn blood in one's veins, which also was the reason why the Finns were not as good as other honest folk, so that the magistrates gave them their own distinct burial-ground in the churchyard, and their own separate "Finn-pens" in church. Eilert had seen this with his own eyes in the church at Berg.

All this made him very angry, for he could not help liking the Finn folks down yonder, and especially little Zilla. They two were always together: she knew such a lot about the Merman. Henceforth his conscience always plagued him when he played with her; and whenever she stared at him with her large black eyes while she told him tales, he used to begin to feel a little bit afraid, for at such times he reflected that she and her people belonged to the Damned, and that was why they knew so much about such things. But, on the other hand, the thought of it made him so bitterly angry, especially on her account. She, too, was frequently taken aback by his odd behaviour towards her, which she couldn't understand at all; and then, as was her wont, she would begin laughing at and teasing him by making him run after her, while she went and hid herself.

One day he found her sitting on a boulder by the sea-shore. She had in her lap an eider duck which had been shot, and could only have died quite recently, for it was still warm, and she wept bitterly over it. It was, she sobbed, the same bird which made its nest every year beneath the shelter of their outhouse—she knew it quite well, and she showed him a red-coloured feather in its white breast. It had been struck dead by a single shot, and only a single red drop had come out of it; it had tried to reach its nest, but had died on its way on the strand. She wept as if her heart would break, and dried her face with her hair in impetuous Finnish fashion. Eilert laughed at her as boys will, but he overdid it, and was very pale the whole time. He dared not tell her that that very day he had taken a random shot with his father's gun from behind the headland at a bird a long way off which was swimming ashore.

One autumn Eilert's father was downright desperate. Day after day on the fishing grounds his lines caught next to nothing, while he was forced to look on and see the Finn pull up one rich catch after another. He was sure, too, that he had noticed malicious gestures over in the Finn's boat. After that his whole house nourished a double bitterness against them; and when they talked it over in the evening it was agreed, as a thing beyond all question, that Finnish sorcery had something to do with it. Against this there was only one remedy, and that was to rub

corpse-mould on the lines; but one must beware of doing so, lest one should thereby offend the dead, and expose oneself to their vengeance, while the sea-folk would gain power over one at the time.

Eilert bothered his head a good deal over all this; it almost seemed to him as if he had had a share in the deed, because he was on such a good footing with the Finn folks.

On the following Sunday both he and the Finn folks were at Berg church, and he secretly abstracted a handful of mould from one of the Finn graves, and put it in his pocket. The same evening, when they came home, he strewed the mould over his father's lines unobserved. And, oddly enough, the very next time his father cast his lines, as many fish were caught as in the good old times. But after this Eilert's anxiety became indescribable. He was especially cautious while they were working of an evening round the fireside, and it was dark in the distant corners of the room. He sat there with a piece of steel in his pocket. To beg "forgiveness" of the dead is the only helpful means against the consequences of such deeds as his, other- wise one will be dragged off at night, by an invisible hand, to the churchyard, though one were lashed fast to the bed by a ship's hawser.

When Eilert, on the following Sunday went to church, he took very good care to go to the grave, and beg for- giveness of the dead.

As Eilert grew older, he got to understand that the Finn folks must, after all, be pretty much the same sort of people as his own folks at home; but, on the other hand, another thought was now uppermost in his mind, the thought, namely, that the Finns must be of an inferior stock, with a taint of disgrace about them. Nevertheless, he could not very well do without Zilla's society, and they were very much together as before, especially at the time of their confirmation.

But when Eilert became a man, and mixed more with people of the parish, he began to fancy that this old companionship lowered him somewhat in the eyes of his neighbours. There was nobody who did not believe as a matter of course that there was something shameful about Finn blood, and he, therefore, always tried to avoid her in company.

The girl understood it all well enough, for latterly she took care to keep out of his way. Nevertheless, one day she came, as had been her wont from childhood, down to their house, and begged for leave to go in their boat when they rowed to church next day. There were lots of strangers present from the village, and so Eilert, lest folks should think that he and she were engaged, answered mockingly, so that every one could hear him, "that church-cleansing was perhaps a very good thing for Finnish sorcery," but she must find some one else to ferry her across.

After that she never spoke to him at all, but Eilert was anything but happy in consequence.

Now it happened one winter that Eilert was out all alone fishing for Greenland shark. A shark suddenly bit. The boat was small, and the fish was very big; but Eilert would not give in, and the end of the business was that his boat capsized.

All night long he lay on top of it in the mist and a cruel sea. As now he sat there almost fainting for drowsiness, and dimly conscious that the end was not far off, and the sooner it came the better, he suddenly saw a man in seaman's clothes sitting astride the other end of the boat's bottom, and glaring savagely at him with a pair of dull reddish eyes. He was so heavy that the boat's bottom began to slowly sink down at end where he sat. Then he suddenly vanished, but it seemed to Eilert as if the sea-fog lifted a bit; the sea had all at once grown quite calm (at least, there was now only a gentle swell); and right in front of him lay a little low grey island, towards which the boat was slowly drifting.

The skerry was wet, as if the sea had only recently been flowing over it, and on it he saw a pale girl with such lovely eyes. She wore a green kirtle, and round her body a broad silver girdle with figures upon it, such as the Finns use. Her bodice was of tar-brown skin, and beneath her stay-laces, which seemed to be of green sea-grass, was a foam-white chemise, like the feathery breast of a sea-bird.

When the boat came drifting on to the island, she came down to him and said, as if she knew him quite well, "So you're come at last, Eilert; I've been waiting for you so long!"

It seemed to Eilert as if an icy cold shudder ran through his body when he took the hand which helped him ashore; but it was only for the moment, and he forgot it instantly.

In the midst of the island there was an opening with a brazen flight of steps leading down to a splendid cabin. Whilst he stood there thinking things over a bit, he saw two heavy dog-fish swimming close by—they were, at least, twelve to fourteen ells long.

As they descended, the dog-fish sank down too, each on one side of the brazen steps. Oddly enough, it looked as if the island was transparent. When the girl perceived that he was frightened, she told him that they were only two of her father's body-guard, and shortly afterwards they disappeared. She then said that she wanted to take him to her father, who was waiting for them. She added that, if he didn't find the old gentleman precisely as hand-some as he might expect, he had, nevertheless, no need to be frightened, nor was he to be astonished too much at what he saw.

He now perceived that he was under water, but, for all that, there was no sign of moisture. He was on a white sandy bottom, covered with chalk-white, red, blue, and silvery-bright shells. He saw meadows of sea-grass, mountains thick with woods of bushy seaweed and sea-wrack, and the fishes darted about on every side just as the birds swarm about the rocks that sea-fowl haunt.

As they two were thus walking along together she explained many things to him. High up he saw something which looked like a black cloud with a white lining, and forwards a shape resembling one of the dog-fish.

"What you see there is a vessel," said she; "there's nasty weather up there now, and beneath the boat goes he who was sitting along with you on the bottom of the boat just now. If it is wrecked, it will belong to us, and then you will not be able to speak to father today." As she said this there was a wild rapacious gleam in her eyes, but it was gone again immediately.

And, in point of fact, it was no easy matter to make out the meaning of her eyes. As a rule, they were unfathomably dark with the lustre of a night-billow through which the sea-fire sparkles; but occasionally, when she laughed, they took a bright sea-green glitter, as when the sun shines deep down into the sea.

Now and again they passed by a boat or a vessel half buried in the sand, out and in of the cabin doors and windows of which fishes swam to and fro. Close by the wrecks wandered human shapes which seemed to consist of nothing but blue smoke. His conductress explained to him that these were the spirits of drowned men who had not had Christian burial—one must beware of them, for dead ones of this sort are malignant. They always know when one of their own race is about to be wrecked, and at such times they howl the death-warning of the Draug through the wintry nights.

Then they went further on their way right across a deep dark valley. In the rocky walls above him he saw a row of four-cornered white doors, from which a sort of glimmer, as from the northern lights, shot downwards through the darkness. This valley stretched in a north-eastwardly direction right under Finmark, she said, and inside the white doors dwelt the old Finn Kings who had perished on the sea. Then she went and opened the nearest of these doors—here, down in the salt ocean, was the last of the kings, who had capsized in the very breeze that he himself had conjured forth, but could afterwards quell.

There, on a block of stone, sat a wrinkled yellow Finn with running eyes and a polished dark-red crown. His large head rocked backwards and forwards on his withered neck, as if it were in the swirl of an ocean current. Beside him, on the same block, sat a still more shrivelled and yellow little woman, who also had a crown on, and her garments were covered with all sorts of coloured stones; she was stirring up a brew with a stick. If she only had fire beneath it, the girl told Eilert, she and her husband would very soon have dominion again over the salt sea, for the thing she was stirring about was magic stuff.

In the middle of a plain, which opened right before them at a turn of the road, stood a few houses together like a little town, and, a little further on, Eilert saw a church turned upside down, looking, with its long pointed tower, as if it were mirrored in the water. The girl explained to him that her father dwelt in these houses, and the church was one of the seven that stood in his realm, which extended all over Helgeland and Finmark. No service was held in them yet, but it would be held when the drowned bishop, who sat outside in a brown study, could only hit upon the name of the Lord that was to be served, and then all the Draugs would go to church. The bishop, she said, had been sitting and pondering the matter over these eight hundred years, so he would no doubt very soon get to the bottom of it. A hundred years ago the bishop had advised them to send up one of the Draugs to Rödö church to find out all about it; but every time the word he wanted was mentioned he couldn't catch the sound of it. In the mountain "Kunnan" King Olaf had hung a church-bell of pure gold, and it is guarded by the first priest who ever came to Nordland, who stands there in a white chasuble. On the day the priest rings the bell, Kunnan will become a big stone church, to which all Nordland, both above and below the sea, will resort. But time flies, and therefore all who come down here below are asked by the bishop if they can tell him that name.

At this Eilert felt very queer indeed, and he felt queerer still when he began reflecting and found, to his horror, that he also had forgotten that name.

While he stood there in thought, the girl looked at him anxiously. It was almost as if she wanted to help him to find it and couldn't, and with that she all at once grew deadly pale.

The Draug's house, to which they now came, was built of boat's keels and large pieces of wreckage, in the interstices of which grew all sorts of sea-grass and slimy green stuff. Three monstrously heavy green posts, covered with shell-fish, formed the entrance, and the door consisted of planks which had sunk to the bottom and were full of clincher-nails. In the middle of it, like a knocker, was a heavy rusty iron mooring-ring, with the worn-away stump of a ship's hawser hanging to it. When they came up to it, a large black arm stretched out and opened the door.

They were now in a vaulted chamber, with fine shell-sand on the floor. In the corners lay all sorts of ropes, yarn, and boating-gear, and among them casks and barrels and various ship's inventories. On a heap of yarn, covered by an old red-patched sail, Eilert saw the Draug, a broad-shouldered, strongly built fellow, with his head, with dark red tangled hair and beard, small tearful dog-fish eyes, and a broad mouth, round which there lay for the moment a good-natured seaman's grin. The shape of his head reminded one somewhat of a big sort of seal—his skin about the neck looked dark and shaggy, and the tops of his fingers grew together. He sat there with turned-down sea-boots on, and his thick grey woollen stockings reached right up to his thigh. He wore besides, plain freize clothes with bright glass buttons on his waistcoat. His spacious skin jacket was open, and round his neck he had a cheap red woollen scarf.

When Eilert came up, he made as if he would rise, and said good naturedly, "Good day, Eilert—you've certainly had a hard time of it today! Now you can sit down, if you like, and take a little grub. You want it, I'm sure;" and with that he squirted out a jet of tobacco juice like the spouting of a whale. With one foot, which for that special purpose all at once grew extraordinarily long, he fished out of a corner, in true Nordland style, the skull of a whale to serve as a chair for Eilert, and shoved forward with his hand a long ship's drawer full of first-rate fare. There was boiled groats with syrup, cured fish, oatcakes with butter, a large stack of flatcakes, and a multitude of the best hotel dishes besides.

The Merman bade him fall to and eat his fill, and ordered his daughter to bring out the last keg of *aqua vitæ*. "Of that sort the last is always the best," said he. When she came with it, Eilert thought he knew it again: it was his father's, and he himself, only a couple of days before, had bought the brandy from the wholesale dealer at Kvæford; but he didn't say anything about that now. The quid of tobacco, too, which the Draug turned somewhat impatiently in his mouth before he drank, also seemed to him wonderfully like the lead on his own line. At first it seemed to him as if he didn't quite know how to manage with the keg—his mouth was so sore; but afterwards things went along smoothly enough.

So they sat for some time pretty silently, and drank glass

after glass, till Eilert began to think that they had had quite enough. So, when it came to his turn again, he said no, he would rather not; whereupon the Merman put the keg to his own mouth and drained it to the very dregs. Then he stretched his long arm up to the shelf, and took down another. He was now in a better humour, and began to talk of all sorts of things. But every time he laughed, Eilert felt queer, for the Draug's mouth gaped ominously wide, and showed a greenish pointed row of teeth, with a long interval between each tooth, so that they resembled a row of boat stakes.

The Merman drained keg after keg, and with every keg he grew more communicative. With an air as if he were thinking in his own mind of something very funny, he looked at Eilert for a while and blinked his eyes. Eilert didn't like his expression at all, for it seemed to him to say: "Now, my lad, whom I have fished up so nicely, look out for a change!" But instead of that he said, "You had a rough time of it last night, Eilert, my boy, but it wouldn't have gone so hard with you if you hadn't streaked the lines with corpse-mould, and refused to take my daughter to church"—here he suddenly broke off, as if he had said too much, and to prevent himself from completing the sentence, he put the brandy-keg to his mouth once more. But the same instant Eilert caught his glance, and it was so full of deadly hatred that it sent a shiver right down his back.

When, after a long, long draught, he again took the keg from his mouth, the Merman was again in a good humour, and told tale after tale. He stretched himself more and more heavily out on the sail, and laughed and grinned complacently at his own narrations, the humour of which was always a wreck or a drowning. From time to time

Eilert felt the breath of his laughter, and it was like a cold blast. If folks would only give up their boats, he said, he had no very great desire for the crews. It was driftwood and ship-timber that he was after, and he really couldn't get on without them. When his stock ran out, boat or ship he *must* have, and surely nobody could blame him for it either.

With that he put the keg down empty, and became somewhat more gloomy again. He began to talk about what bad times they were for him and her. It was not as it used to be, he said. He stared blankly before him for a time, as if buried in deep thought. Then he stretched himself out backwards at full length, with feet extending right across the floor, and gasped so dreadfully that his upper and lower jaws resembled two boats' keels facing each other. Then he dozed right off with his neck turned towards the sail.

Then the girl again stood by Eilert's side, and bade him follow her.

They now went the same way back, and again ascended up to the skerry. Then she confided to him that the reason why her father had been so bitter against him was because he had mocked her with the taunt about church-cleansing when she had wanted to go to church—the name the folks down below wanted to know might, the Merman thought, be treasured up in Eilert's memory; but during their conversation on their way down to her father, she perceived that he also had forgotten it. And now he must look to his life.

It would be a good deal later on in the day before the old fellow would begin inquiring about him. Till then he must sleep so as to have sufficient strength for his flight— she would watch over him.

The girl flung her long dark hair about him like a curtain, and it seemed to him that he knew those eyes so well. He felt as if his cheek were resting against the breast of a white sea-bird, it was so warm and sleep-giving—a single reddish feather in the middle of it recalled a dark memory. Gradually he sank off into a doze, and heard her singing a lullaby, which reminded him of the swell of the billows when it ripples up and down along the beach on a fine sunny day. It was all about how they had once been playmates together, and how later on he would have nothing to say to her. Of all she sang, however, he could only recollect the last words, which were these—

"Oh, thousands of times have we played on the shore,
And caught little fishes—dost mind it no more?
We raced with the surf as it rolled at our feet,
And the lurking old Merman we always did cheat.

"Yes, much shalt thou think of at my lullaby,
Whilst the billows do rock and the breezes do sigh.
Who sits now and weeps o'er thy cheeks? It is she
Who gave thee her soul, and whose soul lived in thee.

"But once as an eider-duck homeward I came
Thou didst lie 'neath a rock, with thy rifle didst aim;
In my breast thou didst strike me; the blood thou dost
    see
Is the mark that I bear, oh! beloved one, of thee."

Then it seemed to Eilert as if she sat and wept over him, and that, from time to time, a drop like a splash of sea-water fell upon his cheek. He felt now that he loved her so dearly.

The next moment he again became uneasy. He fancied that right up to the skerry came a whale, which said that he, Eilert, must now make haste; and when he stood on its back he stuck the shaft of an oar down its nostril, to prevent it from shooting beneath the sea again. He perceived that in this way the whale could be steered accordingly as he turned the oar to the right or left; and now they coasted the whole land of Finmark at such a rate that the huge mountain islands shot by them like little rocks. Behind him he saw the Draug in his half-boat, and he was going so swiftly that the foam stood mid-mast high. Shortly afterwards he was again lying on the skerry, and the lass smiled so blithely; she bent over him and said, "It is I, Eilert."

With that he awoke, and saw that the sunbeams were running over the wet skerry, and the Mermaid was still sitting by his side. But presently the whole thing changed before his eyes. It was the sun shining through the window-panes, on a bed in the Finn's hut, and by his side sat the Finn girl supporting his back, for they thought he was about to die. He had lain there delirious for six weeks, ever since the Finn had rescued him after capsizing, and this was his first moment of consciousness.

After that it seemed to him that he had never heard anything so absurd and presumptuous as the twaddle that would fix a stigma of shame or contempt on Finn blood, and the same spring he and the Finn girl Zilla were betrothed, and in the autumn they were married.

There were Finns in the bridal procession, and perhaps many said a little more about that than they need have done; but every one at the wedding agreed that the fiddler, who was also a Finn, was the best fiddler in the whole parish, and the bride the prettiest girl.

The Lost Fish Hook

LONG ago there lived in Japan two brothers who were descended from the great Sky-god. The elder brother was named Prince Sea-gift and the younger Prince Mountain-gift.

Prince Sea-gift was a fisherman and had only to cast his line into the sea to catch fish; his brother was a skilled hunter and once in the mountains there was nothing on four legs swift enough to escape his arrow.

Yet in stormy weather the elder brother had no luck with his fishing although Prince Mountain-gift was still successful in the mountains. Seeing this Prince Sea-gift felt jealous of his younger brother's success and said one day: "My brother, let us just change places. I will try my skill in the mountains while you become a fisherman." Prince Mountain-gift was not at all anxious to exchange his bows and arrows for his brother's nets but Prince Sea-gift kept asking him and at last he reluctantly agreed.

So the elder brother took Prince Mountain-gift's bows and arrows and went hunting while his young brother tried his luck at sea. But at the end of the day both of them returned empty handed and, to make matters worse, Prince Mountain-gift had lost his brother's fish hook!

Prince Sea-gift was furious at this and insisted on having his hook back, so Prince Mountain-gift took a sword and from it made five hundred fish hooks which he offered to his brother instead. But his elder brother spurned them saying: "These are no good—I must have my own fish hook back and nothing else will do." From then on Prince Sea-gift made his younger brother's life miserable by repeatedly demanding the return of his fish hook.

One day, Prince Mountain-gift was standing by the sea-shore feeling very unhappy when he found a wild goose caught in a snare. He took pity on the bird and set it free. Immediately an old man appeared before him and asked "Why are you so unhappy?" Prince Mountain-gift explained about the lost fish hook and said "Now my brother won't leave me alone and keeps insisting I return the hook even though I have offered him five hundred in its place. I don't know what to do to please him."

"There is no need to worry," said the old man, "I will help you." So saying he took from his bag a black comb and threw it on the ground. At once the comb became a clump of bamboo. The old man took some bamboo and made a strong basket to which he fastened a rope. Then he made the prince sit in the basket and said "I am going to lower this basket to the bottom of the sea. When you reach the sea-bed you will find a pleasant pathway called the Little-shore-of-delight, which leads to the Sea-king's palace. Follow the path to the gate of the palace. You will find a many-branched cinnamon tree growing by a well. Climb up into the tree and see what shall befall."

Everything happened exactly as the old man foretold. The prince, sitting in the basket, sank to the sea-bed and there found the path leading to the Sea-king's palace. It was a wonderful sight, built entirely of fish scales, with many turrets and tall towers. Before the gate stood the cinnamon tree and up into its branches climbed the prince.

Soon the Sea-king's daughter, Princess Fruitful-jewel, came to the well, attended by her maidens, to draw water.

Looking into the well the princess was startled to see the reflection of a man and looking up she was so struck by the handsome face of Prince Mountain-gift that she dropped the pitcher she was carrying and it smashed to pieces.

Running to the Sea-king the princess cried: "Father, there is a handsome stranger in the cinnamon tree that stands at our gate. By his appearance he seems no ordinary mortal."

When her father heard this he went to the palace gate and asked: "Who are you and why have you come here?" Then the prince answered, "I am Prince Mountain-gift, grandchild of the Sky-god," and he told the Sea-king about the lost fish hook.

The Sea-king bowed low and invited the prince into the palace. There he spread before him a carpet of sea-lions' skins eight deep on which he set a couch where the Sky-god's grandchild might take his ease. The Sea-king treated Prince Mountain-gift with great respect, preparing a magnificent banquet for him and offering him the hand of his daughter in marriage.

For three years Prince Mountain-gift lived in great happiness with Princess Fruitful-jewel in the realm of the Sea-king until at last he began to pine for his home and grew melancholy. When Princess Fruitful-jewel saw this she was troubled and asked: "My lord, during the three years you have lived here I have never before heard you sigh; what is the matter?"

The prince replied: "I long to return home to see my brother again, but without his fish hook how can I?" and he told the princess how his brother had bullied him about the return of the hook.

This the princess told her father who readily agreed to help the prince. A proclamation was sent throughout

the ocean realm summoning all the fish of the sea, broad-finned or narrow, great or small, to the Sea-king's palace and a wonderful sight they made, fierce swordfish, striped tiger fish, strange round fish covered with spikes, great flat ray fish with fire-like wings and tiny whiting moving in swift silver shoals. When all were assembled the Sea-king addressed them and asked "Has any fish here taken Prince Sea-gift's fish hook?" Then up spoke a wise old herring saying, "We do not know but the red mullet has been complaining for some time of a sore throat. It prevents her eating and that is why she is not here." The red mullet was sent for and when her mouth was opened, lo! there was the lost hook.

Then the Sea-king said to the prince "I rejoice that you, a grandchild of the great Sky-god, have visited my kingdom. I shall never forget this honour. And he returned the fish hook to Prince Mountain-gift telling him: "Give the hook to your brother and as you do so say these words: 'A big hook, a strong hook, a poor hook, a silly hook.' Then you must spit three times and toss it to your brother from behind your back. And if your brother still bullies you then, whenever he goes fishing stand on the shore, whistle for a wind and I will raise a sea whose tossing waves will ruin his fishing."

And the Sea-king also gave Prince Mountain-gift two jewels: the flood-tide jewel and the ebb-tide jewel saying: "If by any chance your brother should attack you throw down the flood-tide jewel and the tide will immediately rise and overflow the sea shore. Then if Prince Sea-gift asks your forgiveness throw down the ebb-tide jewel and the tide will fall."

Then the Sea-king called a sea-serpent to take the prince home. But as the prince was about to set out the princess drew him to one side and said: "My lord, our child will soon be born. On a stormy day when the winds and waves are raging I shall come to the shore. I pray you, therefore, build me a house and wait for me there."

Then Prince Mountain-gift mounted the Sea-serpent which bore him swiftly back to his own land.

As soon as the young prince met his elder brother again he tossed the fish hook to him from behind his back with the words the Sea-king had told him to say. But the elder brother was not at all grateful and was as unkind to the the prince as he had been before. So Prince Mountain-gift waited until Prince Sea-gift went out fishing and whistled by the sea shore and immediately the Sea-king raised a storm that nearly capsized Prince Sea-gift's boat and drove him ashore.

The elder brother was furious and blamed Prince Mountain-gift for his troubles and one day he laid in wait and attacked him. Immediately Prince Mountain-gift threw down the flood-tide jewel and a mighty tide arose so that the elder brother was driven to take refuge on the highest mountain. Still the water rose and Prince Sea-gift was forced to climb a high tree; but still the water went on rising until, at his wits end, he cried: "Forgive me brother; I admit my envy of you has made me unkind. You have lived a long time in the realms of the Sea-king and have clearly learned much wisdom there. Take pity on me and save me, and I will serve you for ever after."

At this Prince Mountain-gift threw down the ebb-tide jewel and the waters at once receded and were stilled.

Now, remembering Princess Fruitful-jewel's parting words Prince Mountain-gift had built a house by the sea-

shore thatched with cormorant's feathers. True to her word, on a wild stormy day, the princess came riding bravely to the shore on the back of a giant turtle.

The princess said to Prince Mountain-gift, "Our child will soon be born. I will retire to the cormorant house—do not try to see me until the baby is born."

The prince was very disturbed by these words and could not resist looking through the door door of the cormorant house where to his horror he saw the princess transformed into a sea-serpent.

When their child was born the princess was very angry with Prince Mountain-gift and reproached him saying, "If you had not disgraced me by ignoring my words I should have made the sea and land one realm so that every living creature could pass easily from the one to the other, but from now on they will always be separate." And she returned to her home in the sea-kingdom taking her child with her.

And Prince Mountain-gift wept bitterly at her going and he made a lament:

> Whenever night falls,
> I remember my love,
> With whom I dwelt,
> On the isle of wild ducks,
> Those birds of the far horizon.

The Drowned Bells of the Abbey

SORCHE NIC LEODHAS

Stories of drowned cities and towns are common to many countries. The most famous is, of course, Atlantis. The exact site of Atlantis (if it ever existed) is difficult to tell from Plato's account and historians have located it both in the Mediterranean and the Atlantic. The Azores is the most likely place, but even today there are underwater archaeologists working on a site off the coast of South America that may be the sunken city.

In Brittany there is the legend of Ker Ys—"a city which Paris would be proud to equal"—that sank beneath the seas off the coast of Finistère.

In many of these stories the sound of church bells can be heard at certain states of the tide. Debussy's prelude "La Cathédrale Engloutie" is a musical expression of this idea.

IN the far-off days when the Picts and the Scots were dividing the ancient land of Scotland and fighting amongst themselves to decide who could get hold of the most of it, there came good men from over the seas to settle in the land.

They found places for themselves here and there along the coasts by the sea, and lived wherever they could find shelter, and fed themselves on whatever the earth and sea were willing to give them. 'Twas a hard life, but they made no complaint, for all they did was done for the glory of God.

These men called themselves monks, and what they had come for was to spread the word of God among these strange wild people, who had never heard tell of it before. The monks were learned men and wise in the arts of knowledge and healing. They taught the people and helped them in illness and in trouble. Soon they were greatly loved because of the goodness there was in them.

There was a band of these good monks who settled in a wild deserted place at the head of a deep glen near the sea in the north of Scotland. At first there was only a half dozen of them with a leader they called their abbot. The monks made their homes in the caves along the sides of the glen.

The people of the land were wild and savage and given to the worship of demons, but the monks brought them to gentler ways and taught them to live as people lived in the lands from which they had come.

As time went by, more monks came to join the band, and the people for love of them built them an abbey so that they no longer needed to dwell in caves.

For love, too, in time the people had a peal of bells made for the chapel of the abbey. There were five bells, from the smallest silver-tongued one to the great bell which sent praise to God in deep brazen tones.

The bells were cast in the churchyard of the abbey and made of the finest metal that could be had, by the most skilful smiths that could be found.

Now, in those days there were pirates sailing up and down the sea along the coasts, robbing and plundering wherever they could find prey. What they liked best to find was an abbey, for some of the abbeys had great wealth because of the gifts made to them of money and golden vessels and jewelled cups and the like.

The abbey of the glen was one of the richest, for it had prospered greatly in the long years that had passed since the first monks came. Men of wealth and great standing had sent their sons to be schooled there and had paid generously for the service, and many were the priceless gifts that had been given to the abbey.

The monks of all abbeys lived in terror of the pirates, and those of the abbey of the glen feared them no less than the rest. Still, the abbey was well hidden and hardly to be seen from the sea, for the stones with which it had been built were the same colour as the grey rocks of the glen. Besides that, great trees grew between the abbey and the sea, and screened it with their wide spreading branches.

The wicked pirates might never have found the abbey at all, had it not been for one young lay brother.

The young lay brother loved the sweet-singing bells so dearly that he would have sent their voices to Heaven in praise every hour of day and night. But when it was known that pirates were nearby, it was forbidden that anyone should ring the bells lest the pirates hear and come down upon the abbey to raid it. It was always the pirates' way to seek for an abbey by day, and when they had found where it was, they would steal on it by night and take it by surprise.

As happens very often, temptation was too great for the young lay brother. For a while he fought against it and only laid his hand lovingly but lightly on the bell ropes when he passed by during the forbidden times. But one evening as he was on his way to vespers, he not only laid his hand upon the ropes but, thinking a very little peal would be scarcely heard, he gently pulled the rope of the smallest bell.

Clear and silvery, one chiming note rang out, down to the shore and across the waters of the sea. But hidden from the abbey round a point of rock a pirate ship lay moored, to take on fresh water. The silver note came to the ears of the captain of the pirate ship, who knew at once that the sound of a bell meant there was an abbey somewhere near.

As soon as they had finished storing the water in the ship, the captain sent out a spy to find where the abbey lay. Then they waited in hiding, until the moon rose and lit the way, and soon after, the pirates were battering at the gates of the abbey.

The abbot knew by the fury of the attack that pirates were upon them. He ordered the monks and their pupils to carry away the chests of the abbey treasures, and flee by a small door at the side to the caves of the glen where the pirates would not think to seek for them. He stayed back himself to gather the cross and the vessels from the altar. A brave man was that abbot, for he had no more than reached the little side door with the rood and the holy vessels gathered into the skirts of his robe when the pirates broke down the gates and rushed into the abbey grounds. He heard their shouts of rage when they found the abbey deserted and the treasure not to be found. He heard their cries of disappointment at finding so little plunder, and then heard them shout that they would have the bells since there was naught else worth the taking.

When the abbot heard they were going to take the bells that the people had cast and given the abbey for love, he forgot his own danger. He turned at the door and, holding high the cross he had saved from the altar, he called the wrath of God down upon them all.

"Have the bells!" he cried at the end. "Take them if you will! But they will give you neither profit nor good."

The pirates neither saw the abbot nor heard a word of his curse. Up in the bell tower they were, tearing loose the

bells and hauling them down the ladder from the bell loft
with great clamour and noise.

So the abbot went away from the abbey and made his
way up the glen in safety.

When the pirates had the bells all down, they rejoiced
to have such a pile of metal of a quality so fine and pure.
They were sure of getting a good price for it when they
got it to the foreign ports where they'd offer the bells for
sale. They carried them off to their ship, but before they
left they set fire to the abbey.

When they were back on their ship again, they stored
the bells in the hold and then they prepared to set sail. The
captain of the pirates looked back at the burning abbey
and at the sky, red with dancing flames that seemed to
reach clear to the moon. He roared with laughter and
vowed that he'd never set a grander bonfire nor found
loot more to his liking.

But while he stood there looking and laughing, the stolen bells in the hold began to peal. First rang the silver-tongued smallest bell. Then, one by one the others joined in, and last of all the great bell boomed out its deep-toned song. And the peal they pealed was the death knell!

Then the pirate crew came running to the captain. Near-deafened they were by the sound of the bells. They screamed out to the captain that something was amiss with the ship, for the sails were all set and the wind was stiff and the seas running free, but the sails would not fill and the ship would not move at all. The bells were accursed, they shouted.

So then they ran to open the hold and throw the bells into the sea. But before the crew could lay hand upon the hatches, they flew open. There lay the bells rolling gently from side to side and tolling as they rolled. Before the terrified pirates' eyes the bells began to increase in size, growing bigger and bigger and bigger. The timbers of the ship creaked and strained, but the bells kept on growing until at last the ship could contain them no longer. With a great wild noise of crashing masts and breaking beams, the ship flew apart, and down to the bottom of the sea went pirates, bells and all.

The monks who had been drawn from their caves at the sound of their bells, watched in wonder. They could see the ship by the light of the flames and the moon. When the ship went down, they grieved at the fate of the bells they loved so well. But they said to each other that the hand of God is ever heavy upon evildoers.

Now when the people of the countryside saw the flames in the sky, they rushed to the abbey, fearing that all the monks were dead. Great was the joy of the people when they found them safe and unharmed. In thanksgiving for their safety, they built the monks a new chapel and abbey and had a new peal of bells cast, as fine as the lost ones.

There were five of them, just as there had been before, and all were the same as before, from the silver-tongued smallest bell to the brazen-tongued largest bell of all. And it is a strange queer thing that whenever the new bells were pealed and sent their noble tones over the waters of the sea, there came back from the sea an answering peal. There are those who will tell you 'tis only some odd sort of echo, but the truth of it is that it is the drowned bells the pirates stole, ringing back from the bottom of the sea. Even to this day you can hear them if you listen.

Huldu-folk, Nisses and Sea-sprites

WILLIAM A. CRAIGIE

The Huldu-folk and Nisses are better known as Elves and Brownies and like fairies and goblins are not restricted to land or sea. Nevertheless in the Faeroes and other Scandinavian countries, where the sea is so important in everyday life, these supernatural beings are bound to play a considerable part in the lives of fishermen and sailors.

Huldu-folk are found in the Faeroes. They are tall, dark haired and dressed in grey. They live in mounds but go out to fish or farm like ordinary men. They can make themselves and their possessions invisible, hence the saying when something has been lost that "a huldu has hidden it".

Nisses are little people the size of a small child. They too dress in grey but have red pointed caps. They love moonlight and can sometimes be seen in winter pulling small sledges or engaged in jumping matches over fences. They dislike noise and disturbance which can make them vindictive, otherwise they are friendly and generally well liked. They are often called "goodfellows".

The Dulur Fishing-bank

ONE time in old days there was a famine in the Faeroes; a disease had carried off the sheep, the corn had not ripened, no fish could be got in the sea. The distress is said to have been greatest in Vaago, for it was a long time since they had caught anything at the good fishing-banks west in the sea, or anywhere else— they tried it often but came back quite empty.

On this island, then, a poor man was going about, sad at heart, lamenting his distress; he had many children, and could not see how he was to get a bite to put into their

138

mouths. As he went about in this sorrowful mood, and complained of his hard lot, in having to starve his children and die of hunger himself, he met a huldu-man, who asked him what ailed him that he seemed so heavy-hearted. The man told him how badly off he was, and the huldu-man answered that it was a shame he should suffer such distress, for there was plenty of fish, if they had only been able to find them, and he would now tell him the marks to find the fishing-place by:—"the stream in Dal, the mound on Harda-Voll, the river in Tang,—fish here shall you fang—bitten iron and trodden,—he that fishes not then is fey." When the huldu-man had said this he suddenly disappeared, without explaining these dark words and unknown names.

The man began to ponder over what had been said until at long length he thought he had some idea where the fishing-place ought to be. Old folks in the district knew the names, and could tell him where the landmarks were to be found. There still remained to find out what the huldu-man had meant by "bitten iron and trodden". It finally struck him that "bitten iron" might be the bit of a bridle, and "trodden iron" a horse-shoe, so he took these and made his hooks of them.

This done, all the fishermen of Vaago launched a boat, and rowed out to the place that they believed the huldu-man had meant. The man gave all the boatmen hooks which he had made from the horse's bit and shoe, and they let them down. They had struck the right spot, and had not sat there more than a little while, before the boat was laden with fish almost to sinking. They then rowed home rejoicing, and the bank is still called the Dulur (i.e. Hidden,) after the huldu-man, and is regularly frequented. On their way home, the Vaago men rowed past a boat they did not know, but it was a huldu-boat, the captain of which rose from his seat, and said to the man, "A lucky man are you; well were the words explained and well was the bank found." The boat disappeared from view and was never seen again; but the Vaago fishers were glad to have something to give to their wives and children that evening and afterwards.

The Man from Gasa-dal in the Huldu-boat

There is no level beach at Gasa-dal in Vaago, only rocks fifteen fathoms high facing the sea. The place is thus badly situated for fishing, as no boat can lie under the cliffs during winter, on account of the breakers. This accordingly prevents them from keeping a large boat, as it would be too hard work to drag it to the top of the cliffs, and so the men of Gasa-dal share the fishing-boats of the Bo, and go out with them.

One night, when the weather was promising, a man from Gasa-dal left home to go east to Akra-nes, where the men from Bo were to put in to land, and take him on board. When he came east to Skards-a, he saw a boat rowing in to Akra-nes, and being unwilling to keep them waiting long for him, he started to run down to them as fast as he could. He saw then that there were seven men on board, and an empty place for him on one of the seats, but he could not recognize the men, as the darkness had no more than begun to clear away. He had no suspicion but that everything was as it ought to be, sprang quickly into the boat, and they at once pushed off from the shore. The man sat down in his accustomed place, and put out his oar, but on looking about him found that he knew no one on board, and began to suspect that it was huldu-men he had got among; however, he showed no dismay, and rowed as stoutly as they did.

They held north round the island to a bank on the west coast of Vaago. The huldu-men baited and threw out their lines, but the man from Gasa-dal sat still and said nothing, for although he had brought his line with him, his hooks were at Bo, and he had no bait. The foreman on the boat asked him why he did not cast his line; he answered, "I have no CROOK and no BITE." The huldu-man at once gave him both hooks and bait, and the hooks had no more reached the bottom when he felt a pull, and drew up a large fish, which, as soon as he had killed it and laid it down in the boat, the foreman took and marked, and every fish he caught was marked in the same way.

When they had got the boat laden with fine fish, they rowed home and put to shore at Akra-nes, at the same spot where they had taken the man on board. As he had fished all day on his own account, they threw ashore every fish that had been marked. When he had got ashore, and had received his catch out of the boat, he noticed that he had left his knife in it, and called out to them, "Sharp by thigh is left behind." The huldu-man caught up the knife and threw it at him, but did not strike him, where-upon he cried, "A curse on you, but you are a lucky man." They then pushed off from the land again, and the fore-man said, "Hound that you are, you never said thanks to me for the boat."

It is not good, when huldu-folk are near on the sea or on land (and who knows that?) to name knife, sword, axe, etc., by their proper names, but by other words such as "sharp", "bite", and the like. Neither is it good to thank the huldu-folk when they do one a service, for then they also have the power to do one some mischief.

The Ship Nisses

There had been a heavy storm in the North Sea, and many ships had been on the point of sinking. When the weather had improved two ships met out there, and came so near to each other that those on board could call out and enquire where the others came from, and so forth. At the same moment they heard two nisses shouting to each other from the top of the mast on either ship, asking how they had fared in the storm. The one said, "I have had enough to do to hold the fore-stay, otherwise the mast would have fallen." When the crew looked up to see where the voice came from, the nisse let go the stay, which fell to the deck, and then he began to laugh with all his might. The crew had now something else to do than look for him, as the mast nearly fell overboard, and while they were busy putting it to rights again the nisse saw his chance to creep down into the hold, where they could not find him.

Old Tyge Hansen in Lundo sailed with a nisse on board, and they could tell by him when they were to have storm, head-wind, or the like; at such times he was very busy with one thing or another, went creeping about, and tried to get everything put right. At other times he had his abode in the fore-castle. One time Tyge Hansen was sailing northwards, and had favourable weather; but all the same the yacht would not work with them; they could make no progress with it, and so had to sail into harbour, instead of keeping to the west of Lundo. Next day they had such a storm from the north-west that it was clear that their anchors and tackling could not have held, had the ship been out at sea. The nisse knew this, and therefore kept them back in this way. They had him always on board, but could not see him except by night.

The Sea-Sprite

The sea-sprite is seen after sunset standing on out-lying reefs and when men row out to fish he calls upon them and asks to be taken on board the boat. Sometimes they have taken him on board and set him on one of the seats to row with the others; during the darkest part of the night he can row against two at the least, so strong is he. He is good at finding the fishing-ground when it is not clear enough to see the land-marks, but he grows smaller and smaller as day approaches, and fades away into nothing when the sun rises out of the sea. They made the sign of the cross on him, but as the eastern sky grew redder and redder before the sun, he begged more and more piteously to be let go. One time they would not let him away, but when the sun rose he disappeared, and his pelvis was left lying on the seat, for the sea-sprite is said to take to himself a human pelvis, and this is left behind if the sprite himself disappear. He can also produce ocular deceptions; sometimes he seems like a man, sometimes like a dog. He is of a dark-red colour, and hoots and howls so that it can be heard a far way off. Fire flies from when he is on shore. He has only one foot (or tail), but can hop a long way with it, and his tracks have been seen in the snow. When he meets a man on land he tries to drive him out into the sea.

The Tide-Mouse

If a person wishes to get money that will never come to an end, one way is to produce a tide-mouse, which is got in this way. The person takes the hair of a chaste maiden, and out of it weaves a net with meshes small enough to catch a mouse. This net must be laid in a place where the person knows that there is treasure at the bottom of the sea, for the tide-mouse will only be found where there is silver or gold. The net need not lie more than one night, if the spot is rightly chosen, and the mouse will be found in it in the morning. The man then takes the mouse home with him, and puts it wherever he wishes to keep it. Some say it should be kept in a wheat-bushel, others say in a small box; it must have wheat to eat and maiden's hair to lie upon. Care must be taken not to let it escape, for it always wants to get into the sea. Next, some money must be stolen and laid in the hair beneath the mouse, and it then draws money out of the sea, to the same amount every day as the coin that was placed under it; but one must never be taken, otherwise it will bring no more. One who has such a mouse must be careful to dispose of it to another, or put back into the sea, before it dies, otherwise he may suffer great harm. If the man dies, the mouse returns to the sea itself, and causes great storms on sea and land; these are known as "mouse-storms".

Blue Men of the Minch

DONALD A. MACKENZIE

THE Blue Men are found only in the Minch, and chiefly in the strait which lies between the Island of Lewis and the Shant Isles (the charmed islands), and is called the "Seastream of the Blue Men". They are not giants, like the Nimble Men, but of human size, and they have great strength. By day and by night they swim round and between the Shant Isles, and the sea there is never at rest. The Blue Men wear blue caps and have grey faces which appear above the waves that they raise with their long restless arms. In summer weather they skim lightly below the surface, but when the wind is high they revel in the storm and swim with heads erect, splashing the waters with mad delight. Sometimes they are seen floating from the waist out of the sea, and sometimes turning round like porpoises as they dive.

Here is a boatman's song about the Blue Men:

> When the tide is at the turning and the wind is
>   fast asleep,
> And not a wave is curling on the wide, blue deep,

Oh, the waters will be churning in the stream that
    never smiles,
Where the Blue Men are splashing round the
    charmed isles.

As the summer wind goes droning o'er the sun-
    bright seas,
And the Minch is all a-dazzle to the Hebrides,
They will skim along like salmon—you can see
    their shoulders gleam,
And the flashing of their fingers in the Blue Men's
    Stream.

But when the blast is raving and the wild tide
    races,
The Blue Men are breast-high with foam-grey
    faces;
They'll plunge along with fury while they sweep
    the spray behind,
Oh, they'll bellow o'er the billows and wail upon
    the wind.

And if my boat be storm-toss'd and beating for
    the bay,
They'll be howling and growling as they drench
    it with the spray—
For they'd like to heel it over to their laughter
    when it lists,
Or crack the keel between them, or stave it with
    their fists.

Oh, weary on the Blue Men, their anger and their
    wiles!
The whole day long, the whole night long, they're
    splashing round the isles;

They'll follow every fisher—ah! they'll haunt the
    fisher's dream—
When billows toss, Oh, who would cross the
    Blue Men's Stream!

In days of old the "Blue Men's Stream" was sometimes
called "The Current of Destruction" because so many
ships were swamped in it. The people blamed the Blue
Men, who dwelt in caves, they said, at the bottom of the
sea. Their sentinels were always on the look-out, and
when a vessel came in sight, word was sent to the men in
the caves to come up. Sailors were afraid of them, and
many sailed round the Shant Islands instead of taking the
short cut between these and the big Island of Lewis.

When the chief of the Blue Men had all his men gathered
about him, ready to attack a ship, he rose high in the
water and shouted to the skipper two lines of poetry, and
if the skipper did not reply at once by adding two lines to
complete the verse, the Blue Men seized the ship and upset
it. Many a ship was lost in days of old because the skipper
had no skill at verse.

True is the Gaelic saying, however: "There comes with
time what comes not with weather."

One day, when the wind was high and the billows
rough and angry, the Blue Men saw a stately ship coming
towards their sea-stream under white sails. Royally she
cleft her way through the waves. The sentinels called to
the blue fellows who were on the sea floor, and as they
rose they wondered to see the keel pass overhead so
swiftly. Some seized it and shook it as if to try their
strength, and were astonished to find it so steady and
heavy. It carried on straight as a spear in flight.

The chief of the Blue Men bobbed up in front of the ship, and, when waist-high among the tumbling waves, shouted to the skipper:

> Man of the black cap, what do you say
> As your proud ship cleaves the brine?

No sooner were the words spoken than the skipper answered:

> My speedy ship takes the shortest way,
> And I'll follow you line by line.

This was at once an answer and a challenge, and the chief of the Blue Men cried angrily:

My men are eager, my men are ready
    To drag you below the waves—

The skipper answered defiantly in a loud voice:

My ship is speedy, my ship is steady,
    If it sank it would wreck your caves.

The chief of the Blue Men was worsted. Never before had a seaman answered him so promptly and so well. He had no power to injure the ship, because the skipper was as good a bard as he was himself, and he knew that if he went on shouting half-verses until the storm spent itself the skipper would always complete them. He signalled to his followers to dive; and down below the wave ridges they all vanished, like birds that dive for fish. The big ship went proudly and safely under snow-white, wind-tight sails while:

The sea-wind through the cordage sang
    With high and wintry merriment.

Once upon a time some fishermen who were crossing the "Sea-Stream of the Blue Men" in calm weather found one of the blue fellows sleeping on the surface. They seized him, and, lifting him into the boat, bound him tightly with a rope. He slept so soundly that although the fishermen let him fall out of their hands he did not awake.

They resolved to take him to the shore, but they had not gone far when two Blue Men bobbed above the clear waters and shouted:

Duncan will be one, Donald will be two,
    Will you need another ere you reach the shore?

The skipper of the boat was about to shout two lines in reply, but, before he could speak, the Blue Man in the boat opened his eyes, and with a quick movement he snapped the rope that bound him as easily as if it had been only oat straw, and answered:

Duncan's voice I hear, Donald too is near,
But no need of helpers has strong Ian More.

As he spoke he leapt out of the boat into the sea. That was how the fishermen came to know that all the Blue Men have names of their own.

Mother Carey

(as told me by the Bo'sun)

JOHN MASEFIELD

Mother Carey is the wife of Davy Jones and both of them are strictly sailors'
deities. "Davy Jones' locker" is of course the sea, so to go to Davy Jones'
locker is a sailor's euphemism for drowning. There is very little more to be
said since there is no tradition of stories about the couple. Like the fighter
pilots' "gremlins" of the Second World War, they represented the seaman's
attempt to cope with the dangers of the sea by personalizing them.

Stormy petrels are often known as Mother Carey's chickens and are believed
to be the spirits of dead mariners.

Mother Carey? She's the mother o' the witches
   'N' all them sort o' rips;
She's a fine gell to look at, but the hitch is,
   She's a sight too fond of ships.
She lives upon a iceberg to the norred,
   'N' her man he's Davy Jones,
'N' she combs the weeds upon her forred
   With pore drowned sailors' bones.

She's the mother o' the wrecks, 'n' the mother
   Of all big winds as blows;
She's up to some deviltry or other
   When it storms, or sleets, or snows.
The noise of the wind's her screamin',
   'I'm arter a plump, young, fine,
Brass-buttoned, beefy-ribbed young seam'n
   So as me 'n' my mate kin dine.'

She's a hungry old rip 'n' a cruel
　　For sailor-men like we,
She's give a many mariners the gruel
　　'N' a long sleep under sea.
She's the blood o' many a crew upon her
　　'N' the bones of many a wreck,
'N' she's barnacles a-growin' on her
　　'N' shark's teeth round her neck.

I ain't never had no schoolin'
　　Nor read no books like you,
But I knows 't ain't healthy to be foolin'
　　With that there gristly two.
You're young, you thinks, 'n' you're lairy.
　　But if you're to make old bones,
Steer clear, I says, o' Mother Carey
　　'N' that there Davy Jones.

The Flying Dutchman

AUGUSTE JAL

The story of the Flying Dutchman on which Wagner based his famous opera first appears in print in Scenes de la Vie Maritime *collected by Auguste Jal. The tale is very crudely told in the original French and I have adapted it slightly in my translation, although it still reads rather badly. In Jal's version the captain is not named but traditionally he is known as Vanderdecken. Captain Marryat used the legend in his novel* The Phantom Ship *in which Vanderdecken's son tries to save his father's soul.*

In Holland there is another story which appears to have some connection with the Flying Dutchman legend. It concerns a nobleman named Falkenberg who murdered his brother and his bride in a fit of rage and was condemned to exile. On arriving at the sea shore he found a boat with a man in it who said "Expectamus te". Falkenberg was taken aboard a phantom ship accompanied by his good and bad angel. There he remains while the two spirits play dice for his soul. For six hundred years the ship has wandered the seas and mariners still see her in the North Sea sailing without a helmsman, she is painted grey, has coloured sails, a pale flag and no crew. Flames issue from the masthead at night.

LONG ago there lived a ship's captain who believed in neither God nor his Saints. They say he was a Dutchman, not that it matters where he came from. One day this Captain set sail to the South. All went well until he neared the Cape of Good Hope where he ran into a storm of such fury that it defies description. The wind would have blown the horns off a bull!

The ship was in great danger and the sailors and passengers began to implore the Dutchman: "Captain, we must run for shelter; if you insist on staying at sea we are lost and there is no chaplain aboard to give us absolution."

But the Captain only jeered at their fears. He puffed his pipe and drank his beer with as much concern as if he were sitting in a cafe at home. Then he began to sing such blasphemous songs that it was a wonder he was not struck down by a thunderbolt on the spot.

The Dutchman's crew begged him to shorten sail but the more they entreated, the more obstinate he became and the more determined to keep every stitch of canvas set. Even when the sails blew to ribbons and the masts crashed down the Captain laughed at each fresh disaster as though it were a good joke. And so the Captain mocked the power of the elements, the fears of the crew and the fears of the passengers.

In desperation the crew tried to force the stubborn Dutchman to seek the shelter of a nearby bay but when their leader tried to threaten him the Captain threw the man overboard.

Suddenly a cloud opened and a huge figure descended on to the ship's stern. Some say it was Almighty God himself. Everyone was terrified—all except the Dutchman that is—he went on puffing calmly at his pipe.

"Captain," said the shape, "you are an obstinate man."

"And you are a fraud," answered the Captain; "Blow me, I'm not begging any favours of you. Get out of here right away or I'll blow your brains out."

The divine form did not reply, so the Dutchman took up one of his pistols, primed it, took careful aim and fired. But the bullet instead of wounding the white bearded figure pierced the Captain's own hand. This infuriated the Dutchman and he jumped up with clenched fist but as he was about to hit the venerable form his arm fell

paralysed to his side. At this he flew into a rage cursing and swearing and reviling the Good Lord like a heathen.

Then the presence said: "You are accursed. Henceforward you are condemned to sail for ever without dropping anchor or seeking shelter in any port."

The captain sighed and the figure continued, "You will always be on watch and whenever your eyes droop with drowsiness the point of a sharp sword will awaken you. And since you like to torment sailors—this you shall do for evermore."

The Captain smiled.

"Because you will be the demon of the sea; you will sail endlessly through every latitude and know neither rest nor good weather; you will have nothing but storms and the sight of your ship in the middle of a tempest will bring misfortune to all who see it."

"Amen to that," cried the Captain.

The Almighty vanished and the Dutchman found himself alone on board. The rest of his crew had disappeared.

When the Captain saw what had happened he cursed and swore horribly—but all in vain.

Since that day the Flying Dutchman has always sailed in the heart of storms and his only pleasure has been to bring bad luck to poor seamen. He it is who strands their ships on uncharted shoals, sets them on a false course that ends in shipwreck.

No one knows for sure what the Dutchman's ship looks like for it is continually changing its colour and shape. Sometimes it appears black from truck to keel and rigged like a swift privateer; sometimes it takes the form of a slow heavy dutch barge, its great round stern dragging in the water despite the wind's fury.

It is said that if the Flying Dutchman meets a ship and

comes on board his visit is followed by mutiny amongst the crew, whilst the wine goes sour and the food rotten. Again, if the Dutchman asks the master of another ship to take home letters for him and the unsuspecting wretch agrees he is lost: he will go mad and his ship will be swallowed up by the sea.

Why the Sea is Salt

P. C. ASBJÖRNSEN and J. I. MOE

ONCE on a time, but it was a long, long time ago, there were two brothers, one rich and one poor. Now, one Christmas eve, the poor one hadn't so much as a crumb in the house, either of meat or bread, so he went to his brother to ask him for something to keep Christmas with, in God's name. It was not the first time his brother had been forced to help him, and you may fancy he wasn't very glad to see his face, but he said—

"If you will do what I ask you to do, I'll give you a whole flitch of bacon."

So the poor brother said he would do anything, and was full of thanks.

"Well, here is the flitch," said the rich brother, "and now go straight to Hell."

"What I have given my word to do, I must stick to," said the other; so he took the flitch and set off. He walked the whole day, and at dusk he came to a place where he saw a very bright light.

"Maybe this is the place," said the man to himself. So he turned aside, and the first thing he saw was an old, old man, with a long white beard, who stood in an outhouse, hewing wood for the Christmas fire.

"Good even," said the man with the flitch.

"The same to you; whither are you going so late?" said the man.

"Oh, I'm going to Hell, if I only knew the right way," answered the poor man.

"Well, you're not far wrong, for this is Hell," said the old man; "when you get inside they will be all for buying your flitch, for meat is scarce in Hell; but mind, you don't sell it unless you get the hand-quern which stands behind the door for it. When you come out, I'll teach you how to handle the quern, for it's good to grind almost anything."

So the man with the flitch thanked the other for his good advice, and gave a great knock at the Devil's door.

When he got in, everything went just as the old man had said. All the devils, great and small, came swarming up to him like ants round an anthill, and each tried to outbid the other for the flitch.

"Well!" said the man, "by rights my old dame and I ought to have this flitch for our Christmas dinner; but since you have all set your hearts on it, I suppose I must give it up to you; but if I sell it at all, I'll have for it that quern behind the door yonder."

At first the Devil wouldn't hear of such a bargain, and chaffered and haggled with the man; but he stuck to what he said, and at last the Devil had to part with his quern. When the man got out into the yard, he asked the old woodcutter how he was to handle the quern; and after he had learned to use it, he thanked the old man and went off home as fast as he could, but still the clock had struck twelve on Christmas eve before he reached his own door.

"Wherever in the world have you been?" said his old dame; "here have I sat hour after hour waiting and watching, without so much as two sticks to lay together under the Christmas broth."

"Oh!" said the man, "I couldn't get back before, for I

had to go a long way first for one thing, and then for
another; but now you shall see what you shall see."

So he put the quern on the table, and bade it first of all
grind lights, then a table-cloth, then meat, then ale, and
so on till they had got everything that was nice for Christmas fare. He had only to speak the word, and the quern
ground out what he wanted. The old dame stood by
blessing her stars, and kept on asking where he had got
this wonderful quern, but he wouldn't tell her.

"It's all one where I got it from; you see the quern is a
good one, and the mill-stream never freezes, that's
enough."

So he ground meat and drink and dainties enough to
last out till Twelfth Day, and on the third day he asked

all his friends and kin to his house, and gave a great feast. Now, when his rich brother saw all that was on the table, and all that was behind in the larder, he grew quite spiteful and wild, for he couldn't bear that his brother should have anything.

"'Twas only on Christmas eve," he said to the rest, "he was in such straits that he came and asked for a morsel of food in God's name, and now he gives a feast as if he were count or king"; and he turned to his brother and said—

"But whence, in Hell's name, have you got all this wealth?"

"From behind the door," answered the owner of the quern, for he didn't care to let the cat out of the bag. But later on the evening, when he had got a drop too much, he could keep his secret no longer, and brought out the quern and said—

"There, you see what has gotten me all this wealth;" and so he made the quern grind all kind of things. When his brother saw it, he set his heart on having the quern, and, after a deal of coaxing, he got it; but had to pay three hundred dollars for it, and his brother bargained to keep it till hay-harvest, for he thought, if I keep it till then, I can make it grind meat and drink that will last for years. So you may fancy the quern didn't grow rusty for want of work, and when hay-harvest came, the rich brother got it, but the other took care not to teach him how to handle it.

It was evening when the rich brother got the quern home, and next morning he told his wife to go out into the hay-field and toss, while the mowers cut the grass, and he would stay at home and get the dinner ready. So, when dinner-time drew near, he put the quern on the kitchen table and said—

"Grind herrings and broth, and grind them good and fast."

So the quern began to grind herrings and broth; first of all, all the dishes full, then all the tubs full, and so on till the kitchen floor was quite covered. Then the man twisted and twirled at the quern to get it to stop, but for all his twisting and fingering the quern went on grinding, and in a little while the broth rose so high that the man was like to drown. So he threw open the kitchen door and ran into the parlour, but it wasn't long before the quern had ground the parlour full too, and it was only at the risk of his life that the man could get hold of the latch of the house door through the stream of broth. When he got the door open, he ran out and set off down the road, with the stream of herrings and broth at his heels, roaring like a waterfall over the whole farm.

Now, his old dame, who was in the field tossing hay, thought it a long time to dinner, and at last she said—

"Well! though the master doesn't call us home, we may as well go. Maybe he finds it hard work to boil the broth, and will be glad of my help."

The men were willing enough, so they sauntered homewards; but just as they had got a little way up the hill, what should they meet but herrings, and broth, and bread all running and dashing, and splashing together in a stream, and the master himself running before them for his life, and as he passed them he bawled out,—"Would to heaven each of you had a hundred throats! but take care you're not drowned in the broth."

Away he went, as though the Evil One were at his heels, to his brother's house, and begged him for God's sake to take back the quern that instant; for, said he—

"If it grinds only one hour more, the whole parish will be swallowed up by herrings and broth."

But his brother wouldn't hear of taking it back till the other paid down three hundred dollars more.

So the poor brother got both the money and the quern, and it wasn't long before he set up a farm-house far finer than the one in which his brother lived, and with the quern he ground so much gold that he covered it with plates of gold; and as the farm lay by the sea-side, the golden house gleamed and glistened far away over the sea. All who sailed by put ashore to see the rich man in the golden house, and to see the wonderful quern, the fame of which spread far and wide, till there was nobody who hadn't heard tell of it.

So one day there came a skipper who wanted to see the

quern; and the first thing he asked was if it could grind salt.

"Grind salt!" said the owner; "I should just think it could. It can grind anything."

When the skipper heard that, he said he must have the quern, cost what it would; for if he only had it, he thought he should be rid of his long voyages across stormy seas for a lading of salt. Well, at first the man wouldn't hear of parting with the quern; but the skipper begged and prayed so hard, that at last he let him have it, but he had to pay many, many thousand dollars for it. Now, when the skipper had got the quern on his back, he soon made off with it, for he was afraid lest the man should change his mind; so he had no time to ask how to handle the quern, but got on board his ship as fast as he could, and set sail. When he had sailed a good way off, he brought the quern on deck and said—

"Grind salt, and grind both good and fast."

Well, the quern began to grind salt so that it poured out like water; and when the skipper had got the ship full, he wished to stop the quern, but whichever way he turned it, and however much he tried, it was no good; the quern kept grinding on, and the heap of salt grew higher and higher, and at last down sunk the ship.

There lies the quern at the bottom of the sea, and grinds away at this very day, and that's why the sea is salt.

The Sea King's Gift

ANDREW LANG

The best known of all the sea gods is the Roman deity Neptune, easily identi-fied by the trident he always carries. Neptune it is who traditionally appears at crossing-the-line ceremonies to initiate those unfortunate passengers who have never crossed the equator before. Most of Neptune's attributes derive from the Greek god Poseidon whose anger pursued Odysseus so relentlessly in Homer's Odyssey.

But, of course, there were other gods of the sea and the following story is about one named "Ahte" who figures in an epic poem of the Finno-Ugric races called the "Kalevala". Not surprisingly he has much in common with his classical counterparts.

THERE was once a fisherman who was called Salmon, and his Christian name was Matte. He lived by the shore of the big sea; where else could he live? He had a wife called Maie; could you find a better name for her? In winter they dwelt in a little cottage by the shore, but in spring they flitted to a red rock out in the sea and stayed there the whole summer until it was autumn. The cottage on the rock was even smaller than the other; it had a wooden bolt instead of an iron lock to the door, a stone hearth, a flagstaff, and a weather-cock on the roof.

The rock was called Ahtola, and was not larger than the market-place of a town. Between the crevices there grew a little rowan tree and four alder bushes. Heaven only knows how they ever came there; perhaps they were brought

165

by the winter storms. Besides that, there flourished some tufts of velvety grass, some scattered reeds, two plants of yellow herb called tansy, four of a red flower, and a pretty white one; but the treasures of the rock consisted of three roots of garlic, which Maie had put in a cleft. Rock walls sheltered them on the north side, and the sun shone on them on the south. This does not seem much, but it sufficed Maie for a herb plot.

All good things go in threes, so Matte and his wife fished for salmon in spring, for herring in summer, and for cod in the winter. When on Saturdays the weather was fine and the wind favourable, they sailed to the nearest town, sold their fish, and went to church on Sunday. But it often happened that for weeks at a time they were quite alone on the rock Ahtola, and had nothing to look at except their little yellow-brown dog, which bore the grand name of Prince, their grass tufts, their bushes and blooms, the sea bays and fish, a stormy sky and the blue, white-crested waves. For the rock lay far away from the land, and there were no green islets or human habitations for miles around, only here and there appeared a rock of the same red stone as Ahtola, besprinkled day and night with the ocean spray.

Matte and Maie were industrious, hard-working folk, happy and contented in their poor hut, and they thought themselves rich when they were able to salt as many casks of fish as they required for winter and yet have some left over with which to buy tobacco for the old man, and a pound or two of coffee for his wife, with plenty of burned corn and chicory in it to give it a flavour. Besides that, they had bread, butter, fish, a beer cask, and a buttermilk jar; what more did they require? All would have gone well had not Maie been possessed with a secret longing which never let her rest; and this was, how she could manage to become the owner of a cow.

"What would you do with a cow?" asked Matte. "She could not swim so far, and our boat is not large enough to bring her over here; and even if we had her, we have nothing to feed her on."

"We have four alder bushes and sixteen tufts of grass," rejoined Maie.

"Yes, of course," laughed Matte, "and we have also three plants of garlic. Garlic would be fine feeding for her."

"Every cow likes salt herring," rejoined his wife. "Even Prince is fond of fish."

"That may be," said her husband. "Methinks she would soon be a dear cow if we feed her on salt herring. All very well for Prince, who fights with the gulls over the last morsel. Put the cow out of your head, mother, we are very well off as we are."

Maie sighed. She knew well that her husband was right, but she could not give up the idea of a cow. The buttermilk no longer tasted as good as usual in the coffee; she thought of sweet cream and fresh butter, and how there was nothing in the world to be compared with them.

One day as Matte and his wife were cleaning herring on the shore they heard Prince barking, and soon there appeared a gaily painted boat with three young men in it, steering towards the rock. They were students, on a boating excursion, and wanted to get something to eat.

"Bring us a junket, good mother," cried they to Maie.

"Ah! if only I had such a thing!" sighed Maie.

"A can of fresh milk, then," said the students; "but it must not be skim."

"Yes, if only I had it!" sighed the old woman: still more deeply.

"What! haven't you got a cow?"

Maie was silent. This question so struck her to the heart that she could not reply.

"We have no cow," Matte answered; "but we have good smoked herring, and can cook them in a couple of hours."

"All right, then, that will do," said the students, as they flung themselves down on the rock, while fifty silvery-white herring were turning on the spit in front of the fire.

"What's the name of this little stone in the middle of the ocean?" asked one of them.

"Ahtola," answered the old man.

"Well, you should want for nothing when you live in the Sea King's dominion."

Matte did not understand. He had never read Kalevala and knew nothing of the sea gods of old, but the students proceeded to explain to him.

"Ahti," said they, "is a mighty king who lives in his dominion of Ahtola, and has a rock at the bottom of the sea, and possesses besides a treasury of good things. He rules over all fish and animals of the deep; he has the finest cows and the swiftest horses that ever chewed grass at the bottom of the ocean. He who stands well with Ahti is soon a rich man, but one must beware in dealing with him, for he is very changeful and touchy. Even a little stone thrown into the water might offend him, and then as he takes back his gift, he stirs up the sea into a storm and drags the sailors down into the depths. Ahti owns also the fairest maidens, who bear the train of his queen Wellamos, and at the sound of music they comb their long, flowing locks, which glisten in the water."

"Oh!" cried Matte, "have your worships really seen all that?"

"We have as good as seen it," said the students. "It is all printed in a book, and everything printed is true."

"I'm not so sure of that," said Matte, as he shook his head.

But the herring were now ready, and the students ate enough for six, and gave Prince some cold meat which they happened to have in the boat. Prince sat on his hind legs with delight and mewed like a pussy cat. When all was finished, the students handed Matte a shining coin, and allowed him to fill his pipe with a special kind of tobacco.

They then thanked him for his kind hospitality and went on their journey, much regretted by Prince, who sat with a woeful expression and whined on the shore as long as he could see a flip of the boat's white sail in the distance.

Maie had never uttered a word, but thought the more. She had good ears, and had laid to heart the story about Ahti. "How delightful," thought she to herself, "to possess a fairy cow! How delicious every morning and evening to draw milk from it, and yet have no trouble about the feeding, and to keep a shelf near the window for dishes of milk and junkets! But this will never be my luck."

"What are you thinking of?" asked Matte.

"Nothing," said his wife; but all the time she was pondering over some magic rhymes she had heard in her childhood from an old lame man, which were supposed to bring luck in fishing.

"What if I were to try?" thought she.

Now this was Saturday, and on Saturday evenings

Matte never set the herring-net, for he did not fish on Sunday. Towards evening, however, his wife said:

"Let us set the herring-net just this once."

"No," said her husband, "it is a Saturday night."

"Last night was so stormy, and we caught so little," urged his wife; "tonight the sea is like a mirror, and with the wind in this direction the herring are drawing towards land."

"But there are streaks in the north-western sky, and Prince was eating grass this evening," said the old man.

"Surely he has not eaten my garlic," exclaimed the old woman.

"No; but there will be rough weather by tomorrow at sunset," rejoined Matte.

"Listen to me," said his wife, "we will set only one net close to the shore, and then we shall be able to finish up our half-filled cask, which will spoil if it stands open so long."

The old man allowed himself to be talked over, and so they rowed out with the net. When they reached the deepest part of the water, she began to hum the words of the magic rhyme, altering the words to suit the longing of her heart:

> Oh, Ahti, with the long, long beard,
>   Who dwellest in the deep blue sea,
> Finest treasures have I heard,
>   And glittering fish belong to thee.
> The richest pearls beyond compare
>   Are stored up in thy realm below,
> And Ocean's cows so sleek and fair
>   Feed on the grass in thy green meadow.

King of the waters, far and near,
   I ask not of thy golden store,
I wish not jewels of pearl to wear,
   Nor silver either, ask I for
But one is odd and even is two,
   So give me a cow, sea-king so bold,
And in return I'll give to you
   A slice of the moon, and the sun's gold.

"What's that you're humming?" asked the old man.
"Oh, only the words of an old rhyme that keeps run-ing in my head," answered the old woman; and she raised her voice and went on:

Oh, Ahti, with the long, long beard,
   Who dwellest in the deep blue sea,
A thousand cows are in thy herd,
   I pray thee give one unto me.

"That's a stupid sort of song," said Matte. "What else should one beg of the sea-king but fish? But such songs are not for Sunday."

His wife pretended not to hear him, and sang and sang the same tune all the time they were on the water. Matte heard nothing more as he sat and rowed the heavy boat, while thinking of his cracked pipe and the fine tobacco. Then they returned to the island, and went to bed.

But neither Matte nor Maie could sleep a wink; the one thought of how he had profaned Sunday, and the other of Ahti's cow.

About midnight the fisherman sat up, and said to his wife:

"Dost thou hear anything?"

"No," said she.

"I think the twirling of the weathercock on the roof bodes ill," said he; "we shall have a storm."

"Oh, it is nothing but your fancy," said his wife.

Matte lay down, but soon rose again.

"The weathercock is squeaking now," said he.

"Just fancy! Go to sleep," said his wife; and the old man tried to.

For the third time he jumped out of bed.

"Ho! how the weathercock is roaring at the pitch of its voice, as if it had a fire inside it! We are going to have a tempest, and must bring in the net."

Both rose. The summer night was as dark as if it had been October, the weather-cock creaked, and the storm was raging in every direction. As they went out the sea lay around them as white as snow, and the spray was dashing right over the fisher-hut. In all his life Matte had never remembered such a night. To launch the boat and put to sea to rescue the net was a thing not to be thought of. The fisherman and his wife stood aghast on the doorstep, holding on fast by the doorpost, while the foam splashed over their faces.

"Did I not tell thee that there is no luck in Sunday fishing?" said Matte sulkily; and his wife was so frightened that she never even once thought of Ahti's cows.

As there was nothing to be done, they went in. Their eyes were heavy for lack of slumber, and they slept as soundly as if there had not been such a thing as an angry sea roaring furiously around their lonely dwelling. When they awoke, the sun was high in the heavens, the tempest had ceased, and only the swell of the sea rose in silvery heavings against the red rock.

"What can that be?" said the old woman, as she peeped out of the door.

"It looks like a big seal," said Matte.

"As sure as I live, it's a cow!" exclaimed Maie. And certainly it was a cow, a fine red cow, fat and flourishing, and looking as if it had been fed all its days on spinach. It wandered peacefully up and down the shore, and never so much as even looked at the poor little tufts of grass, as if it despised such fare.

Matte could not believe his eyes. But a cow she seemed, and a cow she was found to be; and when the old woman began to milk her, every pitcher and pan, even to the baler, was soon filled with the most delicious milk.

The old man troubled his head in vain as to how she came there, and sallied forth to seek for his lost net. He had not proceeded far when he found it cast up on the shore, and so full of fish that not a mesh was visible.

"It is all very fine to possess a cow," said Matte, as he cleaned the fish; "but what are we going to feed her on?"

"We shall find some means," said his wife; and the cow found the means herself. She went out and cropped the seaweed which grew in great abundance near the shore, and always kept in good condition. Everyone, Prince alone excepted, thought she was a clever beast; but Prince barked at her, for he had now got a rival.

From that day the red rock overflowed with milk and junkets, and every net was filled with fish. Matte and Maie grew fat on this fine living, and daily became richer. She churned quantities of butter, and he hired two men to help him in his fishing. The sea lay before him like a big fish tank, out of which he hauled as many as he required; and the cow continued to fend for herself. In autumn, when Matte and Maie went ashore, the cow went to sea, and in spring, when they returned to the rock, there she stood awaiting them.

"We shall require a better house," said Maie the following summer; "the old one is too small for ourselves and the men."

"Yes," said Matte. So he built a large cottage, with a real lock to the door, and a store-house for fish as well; and he and his men caught such quantities of fish that they sent tons of salmon, herring, and cod to Russia and Sweden.

"I am quite overworked with so many folk," said Maie; "a girl to help me would not come amiss."

"Get one, then," said her husband; and so they hired a girl.

Then Maie said: "We have too little milk for all these folk. Now that I have a servant, with the same amount of trouble she could look after three cows."

"All right, then," said her husband, somewhat provoked, "you can sing a song to the fairies."

This annoyed Maie, but nevertheless she rowed out to sea on Sunday night and sang as before:

> Oh, Ahti, with the long, long beard,
>   Who dwellest in the deep blue sea,
> A thousand cows are in thy herd,
>   I pray thee give three unto me.

The following morning, instead of one, three cows stood on the island, and they all ate seaweed and fended for themselves like the first one.

"Art thou satisfied now?" said Matte to his wife.

"I should be quite satisfied," said his wife, "if only I had two servants to help, and if I had some finer clothes. Don't you know that I am addressed as Madam?"

"Well, well," said her husband. So Maie got several servants, and clothes fit for a great lady.

"Everything would now be perfect if only we had a little better dwelling for summer. You might build us a two-storey house, and fetch soil to make a garden. Then you might make a little arbour up there to let us have a sea-view; and we might have a fiddler to fiddle to us of an evening, and a little steamer to take us to church in stormy weather."

"Anything more?" asked Matte; but he did everything that his wife wished. The rock Ahtola became so grand and Maie so great that all the sea-urchins and herring were lost in wonderment. Even Prince was fed on beefsteaks and cream scones till at last he was as round as a butter jar.

"Are you satisfied now?" asked Matte.

"I should be quite satisfied," said Maie, "if only I had thirty cows. At least that number is required for such a household."

"Go to the fairies," said Matte.

His wife set out in the new steamer and sang to the sea-king. Next morning thirty cows stood on the shore, all finding food for themselves.

"Know'st thou, good man, that we are far too cramped on this wretched rock, and where am I to find room for so many cows?"

"There is nothing to be done but to pump out the sea."

"Rubbish!" said his wife. "Who can pump out the sea?"

"Try with thy new steamer, there is a pump in it."

Maie knew well that her husband was only making fun of her, but still her mind was set upon the same subject. "I never could pump the sea out," thought she, "but perhaps I might fill it up, if I were to make a big dam. I might heap up sand and stones, and make our island as big again."

Maie loaded her boat with stones and went out to sea. The fiddler was with her, and fiddled so finely that Ahti and Wellamos and all the sea's daughters rose to the surface of the water to listen to the music.

"What is that shining so brightly in the waves?" asked Maie.

"That is sea foam glinting in the sunshine," answered the fiddler.

"Throw out the stones," said Maie.

The people in the boat began to throw out the stones, splash, splash, right and left, into the foam. One stone hit the nose of Wellamos's chief lady-in-waiting, another scratched the sea queen herself on the cheek, a third plumped close to Ahti's head and tore off half of the sea-king's beard; then there was a commotion in the sea, the waves bubbled and bubbled like boiling water in a pot.

"Whence comes this gust of wind?" said Maie; and as she spoke the sea opened and swallowed up the steamer. Maie sank to the bottom like a stone, but, stretching out her arms and legs, she rose to the surface, where she found the fiddler's fiddle, and used it as a float. At the same moment she saw close beside her the terrible head of Ahti, and he had only half a beard!

"Why did you throw stones at me?" roared the sea-king.

"Oh, your majesty, it was a mistake! Put some bear's grease on your beard and that will soon make it grow again."

"Dame, did I not give you all you asked for—nay, even more?"

"Truly, truly, your majesty. Many thanks for the cows."

"Well, where is the gold from the sun and the silver from the moon that you promised me?"

"Ah, your majesty, they have been scattered day and

night upon the sea, except when the sky was overcast," slyly answered Maie.

"I'll teach you!" roared the sea-king; and with that he gave the fiddle such a "puff" that it sent the old woman up like a sky-rocket on to her island. There Prince lay, as famished as ever, gnawing the carcase of a crow. There sat Matte in his ragged grey jacket, quite alone, on the steps of the old hut, mending a net.

"Heavens, mother," said he, "where are you coming from at such a whirlwind pace, and what makes you in such a dripping condition?"

Maie looked around her amazed, and said, "Where is our two-storey house?"

"What house?" asked her husband.

"Our big house, and the flower garden, and the men and the maids, and the thirty beautiful cows, and the steamer, and everything else?"

"You are talking nonsense, mother," said he. "The students have quite turned your head, for you sang silly songs last evening while we were rowing, and then you could not sleep till early morning. We had stormy weather during the night, and when it was past I did not wish to waken you, so rowed out alone to rescue the net."

"But I've seen Ahti," rejoined Maie.

"You've been lying in bed, dreaming foolish fancies, mother, and then in your sleep you walked into the water."

"But there is the fiddle," said Maie.

"A fine fiddle! It is only an old stick. No, no, old woman, another time we will be more careful. Good luck never attends fishing on a Sunday."

The Earl's Son of the Sea

B. HUNT

WHEN the Good People fell from the Heavens above, didn't some of them sink in the sea, and there they are dwelling this day.

Many and many a story is told of their diversions and how they be wrecking the ships; but the strangest account I ever heard tell was the fisherman's daughter that met the Earl's son of the sea.

She was travelling the sands by her lone, on the west coast of Ireland, and when she came near to the rocks she heard the notes of a harp. Of course she was curious to know who was out playing in that place and no dwelling near; so over she went towards the sound, and what did she come on only a beautiful yellow-haired man.

"It's destroyed in a short space you'll be," she calls out, "for the tide is beginning to rise and you'll be dashed dead on the rocks."

"Do you know who I am?" says he.

"I do not," she answers. "But you're surely a stranger to these parts or you wouldn't sit there with the waves beginning to rise."

"Maybe I travelled this bay before you were born," says he.

With that she let a laugh out of her.

"I'm thinking the two of us are about the one age," says

she. "So quit your old-fashioned talk and come on out of
that till I show you the way up the cliff."

"You're a beautiful girl," says the stranger, "and the
wish is on me to please you. Climb up out of reach of the
rising sea and I'll play you a tune on the harp."

Well she travelled back over the sand and up by the
path to the cliff, never doubting but the stranger was
following on. But when she looked down she seen him
below on the rock.

"It is drownded you'll be," she calls out.

"Let you not be uneasy," says he.

With that he began for to play on the harp, and the
music enchanted the fisherman's child and the tears ran
down from her eyes. When she looked again to the rock
wasn't the stranger washed from it and a big white wave
curled up from the place.

"I'm after finding and losing a beautiful boy," says she,
and she went away home lamenting his death.

Not a long after she was travelling the sands, and she

heard the music again. There was himself sitting up on the rock as sound as a salmon at play.

"I doubt you're no right thing," says she.

"Maybe not," he allows. "But I'll rise your heart with a tune—if it was crying I had you the last time it's laughing I'll see you this day."

With that he played the cleverest dancing tune on the harp, and he had the fisherman's daughter in the best of humour.

After a while he says, "I'm thinking you have a poor way of living in your home, for it's hard set to earn a bit and a sup that the fishermen are in this place."

"We're miserable, surely," she answers.

"I'll be making you a great advancement," says he. "For I'd have you to know that there's plenty of wealth in my power. Let you quit from your own friends and marry myself. It's a beautiful castle I'll build you, out on a rock in the ocean, and jewels and pearls for your portion to wear."

"A lonesome life," says she, "to be watching the wild birds fly over the waves, and maybe a ship passing by. Moreover you are no right thing, evenly if you have the appearance of a beautiful gentleman. It's a poor man of these parts will join the world with myself."

"Sure I'm an Earl's son of the sea," he allows.

But the grandeur didn't tempt her at all.

"A sea marriage would be no marriage," she answers, and with that she bid him good-day.

"Let your man never travel the sea," he answers, "for I'll destroy the ship from under his feet and leave him dead on a wave."

He leaped down into the water and away with him from out of her sight.

The fisherman's daughter never heard him out harping

again, nor seen a sight of his face. And after a while she forgot the queer lad entirely. Didn't she marry a farmer inland, and it was a comfortable life they enjoyed.

But a notion took himself that he'd prosper more in the States, for he was greedy for gold. He took passage for the two on a great big ship, and away with them from Ireland.

Not a long were they at sea before a sudden furl blast met the ship, and a wave twenty times as high as a house stood up over the deck and broke down. Every person was killed dead and smashed into the wood of the ship save only the fisherman's daughter. She felt the vessel sink down from under her and looked up and seen a beautiful castle rise up on a rock on the sea.

The Earl's son came past on a wave and he lifted her up by the hair of her head for to land her out on the rock.

The fisherman's daughter lived in that place for fourteen years and she lamenting the lonesome hours of each day. She seen the wild gulls flying and whales and every sort sailing the waves. She took no delight in the jewels nor the dresses were stored in that house, and the Earl's son of the sea allowed she grew ugly and old.

It happened one day he was travelling in other parts that herself seen a ship coming down, and she waved a white flag out the window.

A man came out from the ship in a small little boat, and who was it only her own brother Michael.

"Oh sister dear," says he, "is it sitting on a rock you are for fourteen weary years? Sure we heard tell of the loss of the vessel was bringing you out to the States."

"It's a fine castle is here," says she. "But it's lonesome I am for my home."

"I see no more nor a rock and it green with the weed of

the sea," says Michael. "It's on your eyes that there's more in it, for I see nothing at all."

With that she told him the whole story. And he was in dread for to bring her away lest the Earl's son might destroy them.

"I'll tell you what I'll do," says he. "It's back to Ireland I'll sail, and I'll get an image made the down likeness of yourself. When we set that up on the rock himself will believe you are in it, and we may get away."

So he rowed his wee boat to the ship and home he sailed to Ireland. He got the finest image made, and it the dead spit of herself. With that in his keeping he travelled the sea till he came to the rock and his sister still sat there lamenting. But she had a red flag hung out and that was the sign they'd agreed for him not to come near. So he be to wait until she put up a white one and then he knew that the Earl's son was not near.

He got her safe to the boat, and they left the old image stuck up on the rock.

"There's two little fellows like sea-monkeys he's left to watch when he's gone," says herself. "But they didn't see me slip out and they'll never think but the statue is me. I haven't the least fear of them bringing him word there is anything wrong, but if he returns we are lost for he won't be that easy deceived."

They made great sailing to Ireland, and the ship was coming in on the harbour the way they were sure they'd come safe. What did they see only the Earl's son and he riding on a big white wave to catch up to them. The image was with him, and he threw it after the ship the way a hole was cleft in her side and she sank. But the fisherman's daughter, her brother, and the sailors got on shore in a boat before he came at them again.

They seen him from the shore, and he flittering something with his two hands. What was it only the sea-monkeys, and he threw the bits of them up on the shore. He came in himself, but they pelted him from it with stones for his power was lost on the land.

But not a one of that family to this present may venture into the waves, for the Earl's son watches out to destroy them for vengeance and spite.

The Old Man of the Sea

This strange story is taken from the fifth voyage of Sinbad the Sailor, one of the stories from The Arabian Nights. *Sinbad made seven voyages in all enduring every kind of calamity and disaster. He has been called the Arabian Ulysses and certainly one can find some striking similarities between his adventures and those of Homer's hero.*

I know of no exact parallel to Sinbad's horrific greybeard, but ragged, bearded old men turn up on rocky islands both in the Celtic poem The Voyage of Maildun *and in the life of the sixth-century Irish saint* The Voyage of St. Brendon.

DESPITE all that I had suffered on my last voyage I quickly grew tired of shore life. I was bored and restless and felt an irresistible urge to travel again and see new lands.

At last I could stand it no longer: I bought a fine new vessel and loaded it with a valuable cargo, part my own and part belonging to a company of merchants who joined my ship as passengers; then I hired a master and crew and with the first favourable breeze we set sail.

We had been some days at sea when we sighted an unknown island ahead of us. It seemed to be uninhabited and completely barren, yet on the shore, half buried in sand, was an enormous white dome. My passengers were extremely curious to know what this extraordinary white object could be and went ashore to take a closer look, leaving me on board. When they drew nearer they saw that the dome was in reality a giant egg, and very nearly hatched for the chick's beak had already pierced the shell.

The merchants started hurling stones and rocks at the egg, not realizing that inside was a young roc, the giant bird that feeds on elephants! When I saw what they were doing I shouted and implored them to stop for fear the parent birds would return and destroy the ship, but they would not listen to me. Soon they had made a big hole in the shell out of which poured a flood of liquid, down the side of the egg. The young roc could then be seen inside, so the merchants pulled it out of the shell, cut its throat and started hacking great hunks of meat off the carcase.

They were lighting a fire to roast the meat when the day grew dark and the sun was hidden from view as if some great cloud had blotted it out. Looking up we saw that what we had taken for a cloud was a roc, poised between us and the sun. When the roc saw that the egg was broken he gave a piercing shriek to summon his mate and then the two huge birds began circling the ship uttering terrifying screams. I shouted to the master: "Put out to sea, or we are lost." The merchants hastened aboard, we weighed anchor and made for the open sea.

When the rocs saw this they flew off and we crowded on sail hoping to get clear away; but it was not long before the two monstrous birds reappeared and as they came nearer we saw to our horror that each held in its claws an enormous boulder. They flew directly over the ship and the male bird let go his rock. Thanks to the skill of the helmsman, who put the ship about just in time, it narrowly missed us and plunged into the sea with such violence that the ship was tossed high into the air one moment only to sink so low into the following trough that we could see the bed of the ocean.

Before we had time to recover, the female roc let fall an even bigger boulder and this time it hit us squarely on

the stern smashing the whole of the after part of the ship to pieces. The vessel sank immediately and I found myself struggling in the water. By great good fortune I managed to grasp hold of a piece of driftwood to which I clung, paddling with my feet, until more dead than alive I was washed ashore on an island.

For a while I lay exhausted on the beach, but at last I felt sufficiently recovered to set off and explore my surroundings. Imagine my delight when I found that I had been cast up on an island paradise: the trees were weighed down with delicious fruit, there were fragrantly scented flowers everywhere, birds sang sweetly on all sides and there were clear streams of fresh water. Giving thanks to Allah I ate my fill of fruit and slaked my thirst, then I lay down and slept an untroubled sleep.

The next morning as I was walking through the woods I suddenly came upon a very old man sitting by the side of a stream. He wore nothing but a waist-cloth made of palm leaves. Thinking he must be another survivor from the wreck I approached and greeted him. He acknowledged my greeting but said nothing. I asked him how he came to be there but still he did not reply but shook his head and moaned and made signs that he wanted me to carry him across the stream. Thinking that perhaps his legs were paralysed I agreed and lifted him on my back and so carried him to the other bank. But instead of getting down he wound his legs tightly round my neck and refused to budge. I was frightened and tried to throw him off but he clung still tighter gripping my neck with his legs until I nearly choked to death and fell to the ground gasping for breath.

At this the old man stood up and drummed with his feet on my back and shoulders so hard that it felt as if I were being beaten with canes. The pain was so great that it forced me to my feet again, but as soon as I rose he resumed his seat on my shoulders and made signs to me that I was to carry him to the trees that bore the best fruit. If I stopped for a moment or walked too slowly for his liking he beat me so cruelly with his feet that it felt as though I had been scourged, so that I was forced to carry him about the island like a slave. My back and shoulders were rubbed raw for he never dismounted, night or day, not even to sleep; but when he wished to rest he wound his legs about my neck and leaned back and slept awhile. As soon as he was awake again he beat me so hard that I sprang up in haste to do his bidding.

I cursed the day that I had taken pity on the old wretch and resolved never to make the same mistake a second time if I should escape his clutches. But there seemed no end to my misery until one day we stopped at a tree under which lay a number of dry gourds. I took one of them and cutting off the top scooped out the inside and cleaned it. Then I gathered some grapes from a nearby vine and squeezed them into the gourd until it was full of juice. I stopped up the mouth of the gourd and left it standing in the sun for some days until the juice had turned to wine.

Every day after that I used to drink some wine to help me endure the torment of carrying that old devil. The more I drank the lighter seemed my odious burden until one day I had drunk so much that I forgot about him altogether and began to dance with joy, singing and shouting at the top of my voice. Seeing this my tormentor became curious and snatching the gourd from my hands clapped it to his lips and drained it to the dregs. Soon he too grew merry. He began to clap his hands and jig to and fro on my shoulders. Before long he was hopelessly drunk, his legs released their hold and he began to sway backwards and forwards. This was my chance. I managed to loosen his grip from my shoulders and dash the old monster to the ground where he lay motionless.

Without stopping to find out if he were alive or dead I ran leaping and bounding down to the shore where to my delight I met a party of sailors who had just landed for water and provisions.

They were horrified at my wretched state and amazed to hear my story. I was taken aboard their ship where their captain treated me kindly. He congratulated me on a lucky escape for he said I had fallen into the hands of the "Old Man of the Sea" whose victims were doomed to a slow but certain death. The island was well known as his haunt and sailors who landed there took good care not to be separated from their companions.

The next day the ship set sail and I left behind forever that accursed Island and the "Old Man of the Sea".

3

Voyages and Adventures

The Eely-Alley-O

TRADITIONAL

The big ship sails through the Eely-Alley-O
The Eely-Alley-O, the Eely-Alley-O:
The big ship sails through the Eely-Alley-O—
On the fourteenth of December.

The big ship sails too slow, too slow
Too slow, too slow, too slow, too slow:
The big ship sails too slow, too slow—
On the fourteenth of December.

The Captain said it would never never do
Never never do, never never do:
The Captain said it would never never do—
On the fourteenth of December.

The big ship sails too fast, too fast
Too fast, too fast, too fast, too fast:
The big ship sails too fast, too fast—
On the fourteenth of December.

The Voyage to New Zealand

The discovery of New Zealand in the tenth century A.D. by the warlike Maori belongs to a pattern of migration by the Polynesian tribes that had been going on for centuries, scattering them right across the Pacific from the New Hebrides to Easter Island, from Honolulu to the Antipodes.

It is thought that the Polynesians originated in south-east Asia and that they began their travels by hopping from one nearby island to the next. Gradually they spread further and further afield developing more seaworthy boats and more sophisticated navigational skills as they went, until at last they could undertake voyages of thousands of miles that must have lasted months.

According to Maori legend the first settlers of New Zealand came from an island called Hawaiki, which seems to be entirely mythical. Kupe was the first Maori to find "Aotearoa"—land of the long white cloud—as he called New Zealand, but he returned to Hawaiki with the news. Later, after fierce feuding, two Maori chiefs, Tama-te-Kapua and Hoturoa, decided to make a new home in Aotearoa. They sailed in two splendid double-hulled canoes, the Arawa *and the* Tainu.

THE canoes had been launched and laden with stores and Tama-te-Kapua was about to set sail in the *Arawa* when he thought to himself: "My canoe has not yet been blessed. I must find a priest to perform the rites or it will be an ill omen for our voyage."

Just then Ngataro-i-rangi, who commanded the canoe *Tainu*, came with his wife, Kearoa, to bid Tama farewell.

"Ngataro," cried Tama "you are a wise man, skilled in magic, will you come aboard and bless our canoe before we leave?"

"Gladly," answered Ngataro and he stepped on to the deck of the *Arawa* with Kearoa.

Immediately, without waiting for the blessing, Tama gave orders to make sail and the *Arawa* shot away from the land. The wily Tama wanted to have Ngataro with him on this perilous voyage because of his magic powers.

Ngataro was very distressed at being parted from his own canoe and he implored Tama to shorten sail so that the *Tainu* could catch up, but Tama only replied:

"Your canoe is faster than mine, it will soon overtake us," and he refused to take in sail.

For a short while the *Tainu* kept near them but the *Arawa* was faster and the *Tainu* soon dropped astern until darkness overtook them.

The *Arawa* scudded on and as yet there was no sign of land so that after three days Ngataro thought "How fast this canoe travels and what a distance we have already come. Surely we must be near land by now. I will climb on to the roof of the cabin and see if I can get a glimpse of it."

But Ngataro was afraid to leave his wife alone with Tama, so he took a piece of string and tied one end of it to his wife's hair and the other end he kept in his hand. Then he climbed on to the roof.

Hardly had he done so when Tama, finding Kearoa alone, embraced her—but not before he had seen the string, untied it and made it fast to a cross beam. So Ngataro was deceived.

At last Ngataro came down again. Tama heard him coming but did not have time to untie the string.

Then Ngataro knew he had been deceived and asked his wife who had tied the string to her hair. Kearoa answered: "Who, indeed? Who else but Tama-te-Kapua." Then Ngataro forgave her for her honesty but he said: "I will be revenged on Tama."

And Ngataro went and stood on the cabin top and called aloud to the heavens and he raised the winds so that they blew against the prow of the canoe and drove it astern so that the crew of the *Arawa* were terrified and forgot their seamanship.

The next moment the *Arawa* was sucked down into a great whirlpool called "the throat of Te Parata" and it was swamped so that it seemed to be sinking bow first into the maelstrom. The crew were now at their wits' end and Tama cried to Ngataro "Oh Ngataro, Ngataro, do you hear me? The *Arawa* is sinking and so down by the bow that Kearoa's pillow has rolled out from under her head!"

But Ngataro did not answer, even though he could hear the ship's stores rolling from the deck into the sea and the pitiful cries of the sailors as they tried to hold on to the sinking canoe.

At last the cries of the men and the weeping of the women and children moved Ngataro's heart to pity and that mighty man stood up and called aloud once more to the heavens. And the storm ceased and the waves subsided and lo! the canoe rose up from the whirlpool and floated on an even keel again. But although the canoe was safe most of the stores had been lost and little was saved.

And so the *Arawa* sailed on and came at last to land at Whanga-Paraoa (The Bay of the Sperm Whale) in Aotearoa where they found the *Tainu* had already arrived before them, and her crew had erected a temple to mark the landing place.

The Voyage of Cud

JEREMIAH CURTIN

THERE was a king once in Urhu, and he had three sons. Their names were Cud, Cad, and Micad. The three brothers were playing one day near the castle, which was hard by the seashore; and Cud ran in to his father, and said, "I hope you will give me what I ask."

"Anything you ask that I can give you will get," said the father.

" 'Tis all I ask," said Cud, "that you will give me and my brothers one of your ships to sail in till evening."

"I will give you that and welcome, but I think you and they are too young to go on a ship."

"Let us be as we are; we'll never go younger," said Cud.

The king gave the ship. Cud hurried out, and, catching Cad and Micad, one under each of his arms, went with one spring to the best ship in the harbour. They raised the sails then, and the three brothers did as good work as the best and largest crew. They left the harbour with the fairest wind a ship ever had. The wind blew in a way that not a cable was left without stretching, an oar without breaking, nor a helm without cracking with all the speed the ship had. The water rose in three terrible ridges, so that the rough gravel of the bottom was brought to the top, and the froth of the top was driven down to the bottom of the sea. The sight of the kingdom of the world soon sank from the eyes of the brothers; and when they saw nothing but blue sea around them, a calm fell on the water.

Cud was going back and forth on the deck, sorry for what was done; and a good right he had to be sorry, but he was not sorry long. He saw a small currachan (boat) a mile away, and went with one spring from his ship to the currachan. The finest woman in the world was sleeping in the bottom of the boat. He put a finger under her belt, and went back with a spring to the ship. When he touched his own deck, she woke.

"I put you under bonds and the misfortune of the world," cried she, "to leave me where you saw me first, and to be going ever and always till you find me again."

"What name am I to call you when I go in search of you?"

"The Cat of Fermalye, or the Swan of Endless Tales," said the woman.

He took her with one spring to the little boat, and with another spring went back to his own ship. Whatever good wind they had coming, they had it twice better going home. In the evening the ship was anchored among the others again. The brothers went ashore in a boat. When Cud came in, his father put out a chair for him, and gave him great welcome. Cud sat down; but as he did, he broke three rungs in the chair, two ribs in himself, and a rafter in the roof of the castle.

"You were put under bonds today," said the father.

"I was," said Cud.

"What bonds?"

"To be going ever and always till I find the Cat of Fermalye, or the Swan of Endless Tales."

He and his father spent that night together, and they

were very sad and downhearted. As early as the dawn came, Cud rose and ate his breakfast.

"Stay with me; I'll give you half my kingdom now, and all when I die," said the father.

"I cannot stay under bonds; I must go," replied Cud.

Cud took the ship he liked best, and put supplies for a day and seven years in her.

"Now," said the father, "ask for something else; anything in the world I can give, I will give you."

"I want nothing but my two brothers to go with me."

"I care not where they go if yourself leaves me," said the king.

The three brothers went aboard the ship; and if the wind was good the first day, it was better this time. They never stopped nor rested till they sailed to Fermalye. The three went on shore, and were walking the kingdom. They had walked only a short piece of it when they saw a grand castle. They went to the gate; Cud was just opening it when a cat came out. The cat looked at Cud, bowed to him, and went her way. They saw neither beast nor man in the castle, or near it; only a woman at the highest window, and she sewing.

"We'll not stop till we go as far as the woman," said Cud.

The woman welcomed them when they came to her, put out a gold chair to Cud and a wooden chair to each of his brothers.

"'Tis strange," said Micad, "to show so much greater respect to one than the other two."

"No cause for wonder in that," said the woman. "I show respect to this one, for he is my brother-in-law."

"We do not wonder now, but where is his wife?"

"She went out a cat when ye came in."

"Oh, was that she?" cried Cud.

They spent the night with good cheer and plenty of food, the taste of honey in every bit they ate, and no bit dry. As early as the day dawned, the three rose, and the sister-in-law had their breakfast before them.

"Grief and sorrow, I'm in dread 't is bad cooking you have on the ship. Take me with you; you'll have better food."

"Welcome," said Cud. "Come with us."

Each of the others welcomed her more than Cud. The four went on board; the brothers raised sails, and were five days going when they saw a ship shining like gold and coming from Western waters.

"That ship has no good appearance," said Cud. "We must keep out of danger"; and he took another course. Whatever course he took, the other ship was before him always, and crossing him.

"Isn't it narrow the ocean is, that you must be crossing me always?" shouted Cud.

"Do not wonder," cried a man from the other ship; "we heard that the three sons of the King of Urhu were sailing on the sea, and if we find them, it's not long they'll be before us."

The three strangers were the three sons of the King of Hadone.

"If it is for these you are looking," said Cud, "you need go no farther."

"It is to find you that we are here," said the man on the shining ship, "to take you on a visit to our own kingdom for a day and seven years. After that, we will go for the same length of time to your kingdom."

"You will get that and welcome," said Cud.

"Come on board my ship," said the eldest son of the

King of Hadone: "we'll make one company; your ship is not much to look at."

"Of the food that our father gave us," said Cud, "there is no bit dry, and we have plenty on board. If it is dry food that you have in that big ship, leave it and come to us."

The sons of the King of Hadone went to the small ship, and let the big one go with the wind. When Cud saw that they let their own ship go, he made great friends of them.

"Have you been at sea ever before?" asked he of the eldest of the strangers.

"I am at sea since I was of an age to walk by myself," replied he.

"This is my first voyage," said Cud. "Now as we are brothers and friends, and as you are taking us to visit your kingdom, I'll give you command of my ship."

The king's son took this from Cud willingly, and steered home in a straight course.

When the sons of the King of Hadone were leaving home, they commanded all in the kingdom, big and little, small and great, weak and strong, to be at the port before them when they came back with the sons of the King of Urhu. "These," said they, "must never be let out alive on the shore."

In the first harbour the ship entered, the shore was black and white with people.

"Why are all those people assembled?" asked Cud.

"I have no knowledge of that," said the king's son; "but if you'll let your two brothers go with me and my brothers, we'll find out the reason."

They anchored the ship, put down a long-boat, and Cad and Micad went into it with the three sons of the King of Hadone. Cud and his sister-in-law stayed behind on the ship. Cud never took his eyes off his brothers as they sat in the boat. He watched them when near the shore, and saw them both killed. With one bound he sprang from the bowsprit to land, and went through all there as a hawk through small birds. Two hours had not passed when the head was off every man in the kingdom. Whatever trouble he had in taking the heads, he had twice as much in finding his brothers. When he had the brothers found, it failed him to know how to bury them. At last he saw on the beach an old ship with three masts. He pulled out the masts, drew the ship further on land, and said to himself, "I will have my brothers under this ship turned bottom upward, and come back to take them whenever I can."

He put the bodies on the ground, turned the ship over them, and went his way.

The woman saw all the slaughter. "Never am I to see Cud alive," thought she, and fell dead from sorrow.

Cud took the woman to shore, and put her under the ship with his brothers. He went to his ship then, sailed away alone, and never stopped till he came to the kingdom where lived Mucan Mor. Cud went ashore, and while walking and looking for himself, he came to a castle. He was wondering at the pole of combat, such a terribly big one, and he gave a small blow to it. The messenger came out, and looked up and down to see who had given the blow. Not a soul could he see but a white-haired youth standing near the pole. He went into the castle again.

"Who struck the pole?" asked Mucan Mor.

"I saw no one but a youth with white hair; there is no danger from him."

Cud gave a harder blow.

"That blow is harder," said Mucan Mor, "than any youth can give. Go and see who is in it."

The man searched high and low, and it failed him to find any one but the youth.

"It would be a wonder if you are the one that struck the blow," he said.

"What harm," said the youth, "if I gave the pole a touch?"

"Mucan Mor is going to dinner soon," said the messenger; "and if you vex him again, 'tis yourself that he'll eat in place of the dinner."

"Is dinner ready?" asked Cud.

"It is going to be left down," was the answer he got.

When the man went in, Cud gave the pole a hard blow, and didn't leave calf, foal, lamb, kid, or child awaiting its birth, or a bag of poor oats or rye, that didn't turn five times to the left, and five to the right with the fright that it got. He made such a noise and crash that dishes were broken, knives hurled around, and the castle shaken to its bottom stone. Mucan Mor himself was turned five times to the left and five to the right before he could put the soles of his feet under him. When he went out, and saw the youth, he asked, "Was it you that struck the pole?"

"I gave it a little tip," said Cud.

"You have no sense to be lying so, and it is yourself that I'll eat for my supper."

He thought he had only to take Cud into the castle, and roast him on the spit. He went to catch him, and soon they were fighting like two bulls in high grass. When it was very late in the day, Mucan Mor rose up in a lump of fog, and Cud didn't know where he had gone.

All Cud had to do was to go to the forest, and gather twigs for a fire to keep himself warm until morning. It wasn't many twigs he had gathered when twelve swans came near him.

"Love me!" said he. "I believe you are the blessed birds that came from my father's kingdom to be food to relieve me in need."

"Sorry am I that I have ever looked on you or you on me," said one of the swans; and the twelve rose and flew away.

Cud gathered the twigs for the fire, and dried the blood in his wounds. In the morning, Mucan Mor struck his own pole of combat. He and Cud faced each other, and fought till late in the day, when Mucan Mor rose as a lump of fog in the air. Cud went to the forest as before to gather twigs. It was few he had gathered when the twelve swans came again.

"Are you the blessed birds from my own kingdom?" asked he.

"No," said one of the swans; "but I put you under bonds not to turn me away as you did last night."

"As you put me under bonds," said Cud, "I will not turn you away."

The twelve began to gather twigs, and it wasn't long till they had a great fire made. One of the twelve sat at the fire then with Cud, and said, "There is nothing in the world to kill Mucan Mor but a certain apple. For the last three days I have been looking for that apple. I found it today, and have it here for you. Tomorrow you'll be getting the upper hand of Mucan Mor earlier than other days. He has no power to rise as a fog until a given hour. When the time comes, he'll raise his two hands and be striving to go in the air. If you strike him then in the right side in the ribs with the apple, you'll make a green stone of him. If you do not, he'll come down and make a green stone of you."

Cud took the apple, and thanked the swan. She left

down the best food then before him. She had the food
with her always. Glad was he, for he was greatly in want
of it after the fast of two days. She put her own wing and
head over his head and sheltered him till daybreak. There
wasn't a wound on him next morning that wasn't cured.
As early as the day dawned she roused him.

"Be up now," said she, "and have the soles of your feet
under you."

He went first to the pole and struck a blow that took
three turns out of the stomach of Mucan Mor and three
more out of his brain, before he could stand on the soles of
his feet, so great was the dread that came on him.

They fought the third day, and it wasn't very late when

Cud was getting the upper hand. Mucan Mor raised his two arms toward the sky, striving to escape in a fog from his enemy. Cud struck him then with the apple, and made a green stone of him. Hardly had he killed Mucan More when he saw an old hag racing up; she took one hill at a step and two at a leap.

"Your face and your health to you," said the hag, when she stood before Cud. "I am looking at you for three days, fighting without food or drink. I hope that you'll come with me now."

"It's long that you were thinking of asking me," said he.

"I hope you'll not refuse me," said the hag.

"I will not," replied Cud.

"Give me your hand," said the hag, "and I'll help you to walk."

He took the hag's hand. There wasn't a jump that she gave while she had a grip of his hand but he thought she was dragging the arm from him.

"Curses on you for an old hag! Is it little I have gone through that you treat me in this way?"

"I have a cloth about my shoulders. Go into that, and I will carry you," said the hag.

There wasn't a joint in the hag's back that wasn't three inches long. When she had him on her back there wasn't a leap that she gave that the joints of her backbone were not going into Cud's body.

"Hard luck to you for a hag, after all I have gone through to have me killed at last."

"You have not far to go now," said she; and after a few leaps she was at the end of her journey. She took him into a grand castle. The best table of food that he had ever set eyes on was set down there before him.

"Sit there, now, son of the King of Urhu; eat and drink."

"I have never taken food without company," said Cud, "and I will not take it this time."

"Will you eat with me?"

"Bad luck to you for a hag, I will not."

She opened a door and let in twelve pigs, and one pig, the thirteenth, without a head.

"Will you take food with these, son of the King of Urhu?"

"Indeed, then, old hag, bad as you are, I'd rather eat with you than with these, and I'll not eat with you."

She put them back, opened another door and let out twelve of the rustiest, foulest, ugliest old hags that man could set eyes on.

"Will you take food with these?" asked she.

"Indeed, then, I will not."

She hurried them back, opened a door, and brought out twelve beautiful young women.

"Will you take food with these?"

"These are fit to take food with any one," said Cud.

They sat down and ate with good-will and pleasure. When they had eaten the dinner the hag opened the door, and the twelve went back to their own chamber.

"I'll get great blame," said the old hag, "for all the delay I've had. I'll be going now."

"What trouble is on you that you'll be blamed for your delay?"

"Those twelve pigs that you say," said the hag, "are twelve sons of mine, and the pig without a head is my husband. Those twelve foul, yellow hags that you saw are my twelve daughters. The twelve beautiful women who ate with you are my daughters' attendants."

"Why are your twelve sons and your husband pigs, and your twelve daughters yellow old hags?"

"The Wild Man in that house there beyond has them enchanted and held in subjection. There isn't a night but I must go with a gold apple to him."

"I will go with you tonight," said Cud.

"There is no use in going," said the hag.

They were talking a long time before she would let him go. She went first, and he followed. She knocked, and the door was opened. Cud was in with her that instant. A servant rose and put seven bolts and seven locks on the door. Cud rose and put on seven locks and seven bolts more. All began to laugh when they saw Cud doing this. The Wild Man, who was standing at the hearth, let such a roar out of him that Cud saw the heart inside in his body.

"Why are you laughing?" asked Cud.

"We think you a nice bit of meat to roast on the spit. Rise up," said he to a small attendant, "and tie that fellow."

The attendant rose and tried to tie Cud, but soon Cud had him down and tied.

"Bad luck to you, 'tis sorry I am that I ever lost food on the like of you," said the Wild Man to the small attendant. "Rise up," said he to a big attendant, "and tie him."

The big one rose up, and whatever time the small one lasted, the big one didn't last half that length. Cud drew strings from his pocket and began tying them. He caught the Wild Man by the shins, dragged him down, and put his knee on him.

"You are the best champion ever I have seen," said the Wild Man. "Give me quarter for my soul; there is never a place where you need it but my help will attend you with bravery. I'll give you also my sword of light that shines in the dark, my pot of cure that makes the dead alive, and the rod of enchantment to help the pot of cure."

"Where can I find them?" asked Cud.

"In a hole in the floor under the post of my bed. You cannot get them without help."

"I can do anything that has ever been done in your house," said Cud.

With that he went to the bed, and whatever work he had in his life he never found a harder task than to move the post of the bed; but he found the sword of light, the pot of cure, and the rod of enchantment. He came to the Wild Man with the sword in one hand, and the two other things in the other hand.

"The head off you now if you don't take this hag and her family from under enchantment. Make men and women of her sons and daughters, a king of her husband, and a queen of herself in this kingdom, while water is running, and grass is growing, and you are to go to them with a gold apple every evening and morning as long as you live or any one lives who comes after you to the end of all ages."

"I will do that," said the Wild Man.

He gave the word, and the hag was as fine a queen as she was before. She and Cud went back to the castle. The twelve pigs were twelve young men, and the thirteenth without a head was the king. She opened the chamber of the twelve yellow hags, and they were as beautiful as ever.

"I had one son," said the queen: "while he was here he gave the Wild Man enough to do."

"Where is he now?" inquired Cud.

"In the Eastern World, in a field seven miles in length, and seven in width, and there isn't a yard of that field in which a spike is not standing taller than a man. There is not a spike, except one, without a king's son or a champion on it."

"What name had your son?"

"Gold Boot."

"I promise to bring Gold Boot here to you, or leave my own head on the spike."

As early as the day rose Cud was ready, and away he went walking, and very little food had he with him. About mid-day he was at the enchanted field, in the Eastern World. He was walking till he came to Gold Boot. When he touched the body, the foot gave him a kick that sent him seven acres and seven ridges away, and put three bunches of the blood of his heart out of him.

"I believe what your mother said, that when you were living you were strong, and the strength you have now to be in you."

"Don't think we are dead," said Gold Boot; "we are not. We are enchanted and unable to rise out of this."

"What put you in it?" asked Cud.

"A man will come out by and by with pipes, making music, and he'll bring so much sleep on you that he'll put you on that empty spike, and the field will be full. If you take my advice you will not wait for him."

"My grief and my sorrow! I will never stir till I see all that is here," replied Cud.

It wasn't long he was waiting when the piper came out. At the very first sound that he heard Cud ran and caught the pipes; whatever music the man was making, Cud played seven times better. When Cud took the pipes, the piper ran crying into the castle where the wizard was.

"What is on you?" asked the wizard.

"A man caught my pipes, and he is a twice better player than I am."

"Never mind that, take these with you; these are the pipes that won't be long in putting sleep on him."

When Cud heard the first note of these pipes, he struck
the old ones against a stone, and ran and caught the new
pipes. The piper rushed to the wizard; the old man went
out, threw himself on his knees, and begged mercy.

"Never give him mercy," said Gold Boot, "till he burns
the hill that is standing out opposite him."

"You have no pardon to get till you set that hill there
on fire," answered Cud.

"That is as bad for me as to lose my head," said the wizard.

"That same is not far from you unless you do what I bid," replied Cud.

Sooner than lose his head the wizard lighted the hill. When the hill began to burn, all the men except Gold Boot came from under enchantment as sound as ever, and rose off the spikes. Every one made away, and no one asked who let him out. The hill was on fire except one spot in the middle of it. Gold Boot was not stirring. "Why did you not make him set all the hill on fire?" asked he.

"Why did you not set the whole hill on fire?" demanded Cud of the wizard.

"Is it not all on fire?"

"Do you see the centre is not burning yet?"

"To see that bit on fire," said the wizard, "is as bad for me as to lose the head itself."

"That same is not far from you," said Cud.

"Sooner than lose the head I will light it."

That moment he lighted the hill, and Cud saw the very woman he saw the first day sleeping in the little boat come toward him from the hill. He forgot that he had seen Gold Boot or the enchanted hag and her sons. The wizard, seeing this, stopped the centre fire, and Gold Boot was left on the spike. Cud and the woman embraced till they smothered each other with kisses and drowned each other with tears. After that they neither stopped nor stayed till they reached his little ship and sailed away on it; they never delayed till they came to where his two brothers and sister-in-law were under the boat. Cud took out the three bodies, put a drop of the cure on each one, and gave each a blow of the rod. They rose up in good health and vigour. All entered the ship and sailed toward Urhu.

They had only the sailing of one day before them, when Cud recollected his promise to bring Gold Boot to his mother.

"Take the wife to Fermalye," said he to his brothers. "I must go for Gold Boot; the king will give you food till I come. If you were to go to our own father he'd think that it is dead I am."

Cud drew out his knife, cut a slip from a stick; this he threw into the sea. It became a ship, and away he sailed in that ship, and never stopped till he entered the harbour near the enchanted field. When he came to Gold Boot he gave him a drop of cure and a blow of the rod. He rose from the spike, well and strong. The two embraced then, went to the ship, and sailed away. They had not gone far when such a calm came that they cast anchor near shore, and Gold Boot began to get dinner. It wasn't long he was at it when they saw food at the foot of a tree on the shore.

"Who would trouble with cooking, such food as that is on the shore?" said Gold Boot.

"Don't mind that food," replied Cud.

"Whatever I think of I do," said Gold Boot.

He went to shore with one jump, caught the food, sprang back, and laid it down for himself and Cud. When this was done there was food seven times better on the land again.

"Who would taste of this, with that table over there?" cried Gold Boot.

"Never mind it," said Cud. "If the man who owns this table was sleeping when you took it, he is not sleeping now."

"Whatever I think of I must do," replied Gold Boot.

"If you did that before, I will do it now," said Cud, and

he sprang to land. He looked up in the tree, and there he saw a man ready to take the life from him.

"Grief and sorrow!" said the man. "I thought it was Gold Boot again. Take this table, and welcome, but I hope you'll invite me to dinner."

"I will, indeed," said Cud; "and what name am I to give you?"

"The Wet Mantle Champion."

Cud took one end of the table and the champion the other. Out they went to the ship with one bound. They sat down then together with Gold Boot at the table. When dinner was over, the wind rose, and they sailed on, never delaying till they came to the castle of Gold Boot's father, where there was a great welcome before them.

"I will give you half my kingdom while I live and all of it when I die," said the king, "and the choice of my twelve daughters."

"Many thanks to you," replied Cud; "the promise of marriage is on me already, but perhaps Wet Mantle is not married or promised."

"I am not," said Wet Mantle.

"You must have my chance," said Cud.

Wet Mantle took Cud's place, and the king sent for a priest, and a clerk. They came, and the couple were married. When the three days' wedding was over, Cud went away alone. While sailing near land he saw a castle by the sea, and as he drew near he wondered more and more. A raven was going in and out at the uppermost window, and each time bringing out something white. Cud landed, walked up from the strand, and went to the top of the castle. He saw a woman there, and the whole room full of white pigeons. She was throwing them one by one from a loft to the raven.

"Why do you throw those to the raven?" asked Cud of the woman.

"The raven is an enchanted brother of mine, who comes to this castle once in seven years. I can see him only while I am throwing him pigeons. I get as many pigeons as possible, to keep him with me while I can."

"Keep him for a while yet," said Cud.

He rushed to the ship, took his rod, and ran to the loft where the woman was. "Entice him in further," said Cud.

Cud struck the raven a blow, and he rose up as fine a champion as ever was seen.

"Your blow on me was good," said the champion, "and 'tis work you have now before you. Your two brothers are killed and under seven feet of earth in Fermalye. Your wife and her sister are to their knees in foul water and filth in the stable, and are getting two mouthfuls of water, and two of bread in the day till they die."

Cud did not wait to hear more of the story. Away he went, and never stopped till he came to Fermalye. He took the wife and sister out of the stable, then dug up the brothers and brought them to life with the rod. The five made no delay after that, but went to the ship and sailed to Urhu. When near land he raised white flags on every mast.

"A ship is coming!" cried a messenger, running to the king. "I am thinking it is Cud that is in it."

"That's what I will never believe," said the king, "till he puts his hand into my hand."

Since Cud left home, his father and mother had never risen from the fireside, but were sitting there always and crying. When the ship was three miles from land, Cud ran from the stern to the stem, sprang to land, ran into the castle, gave one hand to his mother, and the other to his father.

It wasn't one boat, but boats, that went out to the ship for the brothers and the women. When they came, all spent the night with great pleasure in the castle. Next day the king sent seven score of ships and one ship to sea to bring supplies for the wedding. When the ships came back laden from foreign parts, he sent messengers to invite all the people in the kingdom. They were coming till they blackened the hills and spotted the valleys. I was there myself, and we spent nine nights and nine days in great glee and pleasure.

Sir Patrick Spens

ANON

This fine ballad was first published in Percy's Reliques *(1765). The version I have chosen is taken from Child's* English and Scottish Ballads. *Poetically it is no improvement on Percy's version but it does contain some additional nautical detail.*

Whether or not the ballad refers to an actual historical event is uncertain. In 1281 Margaret, the daughter of Alexander III of Scotland, sailed to Norway to marry King Eric. Many nobles and knights were drowned on their return voyage to Scotland.

Margaret died in 1283 and Alexander III in 1286, leaving Margaret's infant daughter "the maid of Norway" as his successor. She was betrothed to Edward I of England and in 1290 envoys were sent to conduct the young princess to England. She perished on the journey but whether this was in a storm or not is unknown.

Sir Patrick Spens himself has never been positively identified, but one really should not worry too much about the historical background, the ballad has its own poetic truth and that is enough.

Note the bad weather omen in the first two lines of verse 13.

The king sits in Dumfermline town
    Drinking the blude-red wine:
"O whare will I get a skeely skipper,
    To sail this new ship of mine?"

O up and spake an eldern knight,
    Sat at the king's right knee:
"Sir Patrick Spens is the best sailor
    That ever sailed the sea."

Our king has written a braid letter,
    And sealed it with his hand,
And sent it to Sir Patrick Spens,
    Was walking on the strand.

"To Noroway, to Noroway,
    To Noroway o'er the faem;
The king's daughter of Noroway,
    'Tis thou maun bring her hame."

The first word that Sir Patrick read,
    Sae loud, loud laughed he;
The neist word that Sir Patrick read,
    The tear blindit his e'e.

"O wha is this has done this deed,
    And tauld the king o' me,
To send us out at this time of the year
    To sail upon the sea?

"Be it wind, be it weet, be it hail, be it sleet,
    Our ship must sail the faem;
The king's daughter of Noroway,
    'Tis we must fetch her hame."

They hoysed their sails on Monenday morn,
    Wi' a' the speed they may;
They hae landed in Noroway,
    Upon a Wodensday.

They hadna been a week, a week
    In Noroway but twae,
When that the lords o Noroway
    Began aloud to say:

"Ye Scottishmen spend a' our king's goud,
 And a' our queenis fee"
"Ye lie, ye lie, ye liars loud!
 Fu' loud I hear ye lie!

"For I brought as much white monie
 As gane my men and me,—
And I brought a half-fou o' gude red goud
 Out o'er the sea wi' me.

"Make ready, make ready, my merrymen a'!
   Our gude ship sails the morn:"
"Now, ever alake! my master dear,
   I fear a deadly storm!

"I saw the new moon late yestreen,
   Wi' the auld moon in her arm;
And if we gang to sea, master,
   I fear we'll come to harm."

They hadna sailed a league, a league,
   A league but barely three,
When the lift grew dark, and the wind blew loud,
   And gurly grew the sea.

The ankers brak, and the topmasts lap,
   It was sic a deadly storm,
And the waves came o'er the broken ship,
   Till a' her sides were torn.

"O where will I get a gude sailor
   To take my helm in hand,
Till I get up to the tall topmast,
   To see if I can spy land?"

"O here am I, a sailor gude,
   To take the helm in hand,
Till you go up to the tall topmast,—
   But I fear you'll ne'er spy land."

He hadna gane a step, a step,
   A step but barely ane,
When a bout flew out of our goodly ship,
   And the salt sea it came in.

"Gae fetch a web o' the silken claith,
  Another o' the twine,
And wap them into our ship's side,
  And letna the sea come in."

They fetched a web o' the silken claith,
  Another o' the twine,
And they wapped them roun' that gude ship's side,
  But still the sea came in.

O laith, laith were our gude Scots lords
  To weet their cork-heeled shoon!
But lang or a' the play was played,
  They wat their hats aboon.

And mony was the feather-bed
  That flatter'd on the faem,
And mony was the gude lord's son
  That never mair cam hame.

The ladyes wrang their fingers white,
  The maidens tore their hair,
A' for the sake of their true loves,
  For them they'll see nae mair.

O lang, lang may the ladyes sit,
  Wi' their fans into their hand,
Before they see Sir Patrick Spens
  Come sailing to the strand!

And lang, lang may the maidens sit,
  Wi' their goud kaims in their hair,
A' waiting for their ain dear loves,
  For them they'll see nae mair.

O forty miles off Aberdeen
  'Tis fifty fathoms deep,
And there lies gude Sir Patrick Spens,
  Wi' the Scots lords at his feet.

How the Argonauts were driven into the Unknown Sea

CHARLES KINGSLEY

The crew of the Argo was probably the most celebrated of all time, including as it did not only the hero Jason, but Orpheus, Hercules, Theseus and Meleager.

Jason was the rightful heir to the throne of Thessaly which had been usurped by Peleus. When Jason tried to claim his rights Peleus agreed to renounce the the throne if Jason brought back the Golden Fleece which was in the care of King Aeëtes of Colchis on the Black Sea. The King had attached it to a tree guarded by an ever watchful dragon.

The Argonauts, fifty of them altogether, set sail and after many adventures arrived at Colchis. With the help of King Aeëtes' daughter Medeia, who possessed magical powers, Jason defeated the dragon and obtained the fleece. Then the Argonauts, taking Medeia with them, fled from Colchis with King Aeëtes in close pursuit.

SO they fled away in haste to the westward; but Aeëtes manned his fleet and followed them. And Lynceus the quick-eyed saw him coming, while he was still many a mile away, and cried, "I see a hundred ships, like a flock of white swans, far in the east." And at that they rowed hard, like heroes; but the ships came nearer every hour.

Then Medeia, the dark witch-maiden, laid a cruel and a cunning plot; for she killed Absyrtus her young brother, and cast him into the sea, and said, "Ere my father can take up his corpse and bury it, he must wait long, and be left far behind."

And all the heroes shuddered, and looked one at the other for shame; yet they did not punish that dark witch-woman, because she had won for them the golden fleece.

And when Aeëtes came to the place he saw the floating corpse; and he stopped a long while, and bewailed his son, and took him up, and went home. But he sent on his sailors toward the westward, and bound them by a mighty curse—"Bring back to me that dark witch-woman, that she may die a dreadful death. But if you return without her, you shall die by the same death yourselves."

So the Argonauts escaped for that time: but Father Zeus saw that foul crime; and out of the heavens he sent a storm, and swept the ship far from her course. Day after day the storm drove her, amid foam and blinding mist, till they knew no longer where they were, for the sun was blotted from the skies. And at last the ship struck on a shoal, amid low isles of mud and sand, and the waves rolled over her and through her, and the heroes lost all hope of life.

Then Jason cried to Hera, "Fair queen, who hast befriended us till now, why hast thou left us in our misery, to die here among unknown seas? It is hard to lose the honour which we have won with such toil and danger, and hard never to see Hellas again, and the pleasant bay of Pagasai."

Then out and spoke the magic bough which stood upon the *Argo*'s beak, "Because Father Zeus is angry, all this has fallen on you; for a cruel crime has been done on board, and the sacred ship is foul with blood."

At that some of the heroes cried, "Medeia is the murderess. Let the witch-woman bear her sin, and die!" And they seized Medeia, to hurl her into the sea, and atone for the young boy's death; but the magic bough spoke again,

"Let her live till her crimes are full. Vengeance waits for her, slow and sure; but she must live, for you need her still. She must show you the way to her sister Circe, who lives among the islands of the West. To her you must sail, a weary way, and she shall cleanse you from your guilt."

Then all the heroes wept aloud when they heard the sentence of the oak; for they knew that a dark journey lay before them, and years of bitter toil. And some upbraided the dark witch-woman, and some said, "Nay, we are her debtors still; without her we should never have won the fleece." But most of them bit their lips in silence, for they feared the witch's spells.

And now the sea grew calmer, and the sun shone out once more, and the heroes thrust the ship off the sand-bank, and rowed forward on their weary course under the guiding of the dark witch-maiden, into the wastes of the unknown sea.

Whither they went I cannot tell, nor how they came to Circe's isle. Some say that they went to the westward, and so came into the Adriatic, dragging their ship over the snowy Alps. And others say that they went southward, into the Red Indian Sea, and past the sunny lands where spices grow, round Æthiopa toward the West; and that at last they came to Libya, and dragged their ship across the burning sands, and over the hills into the Syrtes, where the flats and quicksands spread for many a mile, between rich Cyrene and the Lotus-eaters' shore. But all these are but dreams and fables, and dim hints of unknown lands.

But all say that they came to a place where they had to drag their ship across the land nine days with ropes and rollers, till they came into an unknown sea. And thence they went northward ever, up the Tanais, which we call Don, past the Geloni and Sauromatai, and many a wandering shepherd-tribe, and the one-eyed Arimaspi, of whom old Greek poets tell, who steal the gold from the Griffins, in the cold Rhipaian hills.

And they passed the Scythian archers, and the Tauri who eat men, and the wandering Hyperboreoi, who feed their flocks beneath the pole-star, until they came into the northern ocean, the dull dead Cronian Sea. And there *Argo* would move on no longer; and each man clasped his elbow, and leaned his head upon his hand, heart-broken with toil and hunger, and gave himself up to death. But brave Ancaios the helmsman cheered up their hearts once more, and bade them leap on land, and haul the ship with ropes and rollers for many a weary day, whether over land, or mud, or ice, I know not, for the song is mixed and broken like a dream. And it says next, how they came to the rich nation of the famous long-lived men; and to the coast of the Cimmerians, who never saw the sun, buried deep in the glens of the snow mountains; and to the fair land of Hermione, where dwelt the most righteous of all nations; and to the gates of the world below, and to the dwelling-place of dreams.

And at last Ancaios shouted, "Endure a little while, brave friends, the worst is surely past; for I can see the pure west wind ruffle the water, and hear the roar of ocean on the sands. So raise up the mast, and set the sail, and face what comes like men."

Then out spoke the magic bough, "Ah, would that I had perished long ago, and been whelmed by the dread blue rocks, beneath the fierce swell of the Euxine! Better so, than to wander for ever, disgraced by the guilt of my princes; for the blood of Absyrtus still tracks me, and woe follows hard upon woe. And now some dark horror will clutch me, if I come near the Isle of Ierne. Unless you will cling to the land, and sail southward and southward for ever, I shall wander beyond the Atlantic, to the ocean which has no shore."

Then they blest the magic bough, and sailed southward along the land. But ere they could pass Ierne, the land of mists and storms, the wild wind came down, dark and roaring, and caught the sail, and strained the ropes. And away they drove twelve nights, on the wide wild western sea, through the foam, and over the rollers, while they saw neither sun nor stars. And they cried again, "We shall perish, for we know not where we are. We are lost in the dreary damp darkness, and cannot tell north from south."

But Lynceus the long-sighted called gaily from the bows, "Take heart again, brave sailors; for I see a pine-clad isle, and the halls of the kind Earth-mother, with a crown of clouds around them."

But Orpheus said, "Turn from them, for no living man can land there: there is no harbour on the coast, but steep-walled cliffs all round."

So Ancaios turned the ship away; and for three days more they sailed on, till they came to Aiaia, Circe's home, and the fairy island of the West.

And there Jason bid them land, and seek about for any sign of living man. And as they went inland Circe met them, coming down toward the ship; and they trembled when they saw her, for her hair, and face, and robes shone like flame.

And she came and looked at Medeia; and Medeia hid her face beneath her veil.

And Circe cried, "Ah, wretched girl, have you forgotten all your sins, that you come hither to my island, where the flowers bloom all the year round? Where is your aged father, and the brother whom you killed? Little

do I expect you to return in safety with these strangers whom you love. I will send you food and wine: but your ship must not stay here, for it is foul with sin, and foul with sin its crew."

And the heroes prayed her, but in vain, and cried, "Cleanse us from our guilt!" But she sent them away, and said, "Go on to Malea, and there you may be cleansed, and return home."

Then a fair wind rose, and they sailed eastward, by Tartessus on the Iberian shore, till they came to the Pillars of Hercules, and the Mediterranean Sea. And thence they sailed on through the deeps of Sardinia, and past the Ausonian islands, and the capes of the Tyrrhenian shore, till they came to a flowery island, upon a still bright summer's eve. And as they neared it, slowly and wearily, they heard sweet songs upon the shore. But when Medeia heard it, she started, and cried, "Beware, all heroes, for these are the rocks of the Sirens. You must pass close by them, for there is no other channel; but those who listen to that song are lost."

Then Orpheus spoke, the king of all minstrels, "Let them match their song against mine. I have charmed stones, and trees, and dragons, how much more the hearts of men!" So he caught up his lyre, and stood upon the poop, and began his magic song.

And now they could see the Sirens on Anthemoëssa, the flowery isle; three fair maidens sitting on the beach, beneath a red rock in the setting sun, among beds of crimson poppies and golden asphodel. Slowly they sung and sleepily, with silver voices, mild and clear, which stole over the golden waters, and into the hearts of all the heroes, in spite of Orpheus' song.

And all things stayed around and listened; the gulls sat

in white lines along the rocks; on the beach great seals lay basking, and kept time with lazy heads; while silver shoals of fish came up to hearken, and whispered as they broke the shining calm. The Wind overhead hushed his whistling, as he shepherded his clouds toward the west; and the clouds stood in mid blue, and listened dreaming, like a flock of golden sheep.

And as the heroes listened, the oars fell from their hands, and their heads drooped on their breasts, and they closed their heavy eyes; and they dreamed of bright still gardens, and of slumbers under murmuring pines, till all their toil seemed foolishness, and they thought of their renown no more.

Then one lifted his head suddenly, and cried, "What use in wandering for ever? Let us stay here and rest awhile."

And another, "Let us row to the shore, and hear the words they sing." And another, "I care not for the words, but for the music. They shall sing me to sleep, that I may rest."

And Butes, the son of Pandion, the fairest of all mortal men, leapt out and swam toward the shore, crying, "I come, I come, fair maidens, to live and die here, listening to your song."

Then Medeia clapped her hands together, and cried, "Sing louder, Orpheus, sing a bolder strain; wake up these hapless sluggards, or none of them will see the land of Hellas more."

Then Orpheus lifted his harp, and crashed his cunning hand across the strings; and his music and his voice rose like a trumpet through the still evening air; into the air it rushed like thunder, till the rocks rang and the sea; and into their souls it rushed like wine, till all hearts beat fast within their breasts.

And he sung the song of Perseus, how the Gods led him over land and sea, and how he slew the loathly Gorgon, and won himself a peerless bride; and how he sits now with the Gods upon Olympus, a shining star in the sky, immortal with his immortal bride, and honoured by all men below.

So Orpheus sang, and the Sirens, answering each other across the golden sea, till Orpheus' voice drowned the Sirens', and the heroes caught their oars again.

And they cried, "We will be men like Perseus, and we will dare and suffer to the last. Sing us his song again, brave Orpheus, that we may forget the Sirens and their spell."

And as Orpheus sang, they dashed their oars into the sea, and kept time to his music, as they fled fast away; and the Sirens' voices died behind them, in the hissing of the foam along their wake.

But Butes swam to the shore, and knelt down before the Sirens, and cried, "Sing on! sing on!" But he could say no more, for a charmed sleep came over him, and a pleasant humming in his ears; and he sank all alone upon the pebbles, and forgot all heaven and earth, and never looked at that sad beach around him, all strewn with the bones of men.

Then slowly rose up those three fair sisters, with a cruel smile upon their lips; and slowly they crept down towards him, like leopards who creep upon their prey; and their hands were like the talons of eagles as they stept across the bones of their victims to enjoy their cruel feast.

But fairest Aphrodite saw him from the highest Idalian peak, and she pitied his youth and his beauty, and leapt up from her golden throne; and like a falling star she cleft the sky, and left a trail of glittering light, till she stooped to the Isle of the Sirens, and snatched their prey from their claws. And she lifted Butes as he lay sleeping, and wrapt him in a golden mist; and she bore him to the peak of Lilybaeum, and he slept there many a pleasant year.

But when the Sirens saw that they were conquered, they shrieked for envy and rage, and leapt from the beach into the sea, and were changed into rocks until this day.

Then they came to the straits by Lilybaeum, and saw Sicily, the three-cornered island, under which Enceladus the giant lies groaning day and night, and when he turns the earth quakes, and his breath bursts out in roaring flames from the highest cone of Aetna, above the chestnut woods. And there Charybdis caught them in its fearful coils of wave, and rolled mast-high about them, and spun them round and round; and they could go neither back nor forward, while the whirlpool sucked them in.

And while they struggled they saw near them, on the

other side the strait, a rock stand in the water, with its peak wrapt round in clouds—a rock which no man could climb, though he had twenty hands and feet, for the stone was smooth and slippery, as if polished by man's hand; and half-way up a misty cave looked out toward the west.

And when Orpheus saw it he groaned, and struck his hands together. And "Little will it help us," he cried, "to escape the jaws of the whirlpool; for in that cave lives Scylla, the sea-hag with a young whelp's voice; my mother warned me of her ere we sailed away from Hellas; she has six heads, and six long necks, and hides in that dark cleft. And from her cave she fishes for all things which pass by— for sharks, and seals, and dolphins, and all the herds of Amphitrite. And never ship's crew boasted that they came safe by her rock, for she bends her long necks down to them, and every mouth takes up a man. And who will help us now? For Hera and Zeus hate us, and our ship is foul with guilt; so we must die, whatever befalls."

Then out of the depths came Thetis, Peleus' silver-footed bride, for love of her gallant husband, and all her nymphs around her; and they played like snow-white dolphins, diving on from wave to wave, before the ship, and in her wake, and beside her, as dolphins play. And they caught the ship, and guided her, and passed her on from hand to hand, and tossed her through the billows, as maidens toss the ball. And when Scylla stooped to seize her, they struck back her ravening heads, and foul Scylla whined, as a whelp whines, at the touch of their gentle hands. But she shrank into her cave affrighted—for all bad things shrink from good—and *Argo* leapt safe past her, while a fair breeze rose behind. Then Thetis and her nymphs sank down to their coral caves beneath the sea, and their gardens of green and purple, where live flowers bloom all the year round; while the heroes went on rejoicing, yet dreading what might come next.

After that they rowed on steadily for many a weary day, till they saw a long high island, and beyond it a mountain land. And they searched till they found a harbour, and there rowed boldly in. But after awhile they stopped, and wondered, for there stood a great city on the shore, and temples and walls and gardens, and castles high in air upon the cliffs. And on either side they saw a harbour, with a narrow mouth, but wide within; and black ships without number, high and dry upon the shore.

Then Ancaios, the wise helmsman, spoke, "What new wonder is this? I know all isles, and harbours, and the windings of all seas; and this should be Corcyra, where a few wild goat-herds dwell. But whence come these new harbours and vast works of polished stone?"

But Jason said, "They can be no savage people. We will go in and take our chance."

So they rowed into the harbour, among a thousand black-beaked ships, each larger far than *Argo*, toward a quay of polished stone. And they wondered at that mighty city, with its roofs of burnished brass, and long and lofty walls of marble, with strong palisades above. And the quays were full of people, merchants, and mariners, and slaves, going to and fro with merchandise among the crowd of ships. And the heroes' hearts were humbled, and they looked at each other and said, "We thought ourselves a gallant crew when we sailed from Iolcos by the sea; but how small we look before this city, like an ant before a hive of bees."

Then the sailors hailed them roughly from the quay. "What men are you?—we want no strangers here, nor pirates. We keep our business to ourselves."

But Jason answered gently, with many a flattering word, and praised their city and their harbour, and their fleet of gallant ships. "Surely you are the children of Poseidon, and the masters of the sea; and we are but poor wandering mariners, worn out with thirst and toil. Give us but food and water, and we will go on our voyage in peace."

Then the sailors laughed, and answered, "Stranger, you are no fool; you talk like an honest man, and you shall find us honest too. We are the children of Poseidon, and the masters of the sea; but come ashore to us, and you shall have the best that we can give."

So they limped ashore, all stiff and weary, with long ragged beards and sunburnt cheeks, and garments torn and weather-stained, and weapons rusted with the spray, while the sailors laughed at them (for they were rough-tongued, though their hearts were frank and kind). And one said, "These fellows are but raw sailors; they look as if they had been sea-sick all the day." And another, "Their legs have grown crooked with much rowing, till they waddle in their walk like ducks."

At that Idas the rash would have struck them; but Jason held him back, till one of the merchant kings spoke to them, a tall and stately man.

"Do not be angry, strangers; the sailor boys must have their jest. But we will treat you justly and kindly, for strangers and poor men come from God; and you seem no common sailors by your strength, and height, and weapons. Come up with me to the palace of Alcinous, the rich sea-going king, and we will feast you well and heartily; and after that you shall tell us your name."

But Medeia hung back, and trembled, and whispered in Jason's ear, "We are betrayed, and are going to our ruin, for I see my countrymen among the crowd; dark-eyed Colchi in steel mailshirts, such as they wear in my father's land."

"It is too late to turn," said Jason. And he spoke to the merchant king. "What country is this, good sir; and what is this new-built town?"

"This is the land of the Phaeaces, beloved by all the immortals; for they come hither and feast like friends with us, and sit by our side in the hall. Hither we came from Liburnia to escape the unrighteous Cyclopes; for they robbed us, peaceful merchants, of our hard-earned wares and wealth. So Nausithous, the son of Poseidon, brought us hither, and died in peace; and now his son Alcinous rules us, and Arete the wisest of queens."

So they went up across the square, and wondered still more as they went; for along the quays lay in order great cables, and yards, and masts, before the fair temple of Poseidon, the blue-haired king of the seas. And round the square worked the shipwrights, as many in number as ants, twining ropes, and hewing timber, and smoothing long yards and oars. And the Minuai went on in silence through clean white marble streets, till they came to the hall of Alcinous, and they wondered then still more. For the lofty palace shone aloft in the sun, with walls of plated brass, from the threshold to the innermost chamber, and the doors were of silver and gold. And on each side of the doorway sat living dogs of gold, who never grew old or died, so well Hephaistos had made them in his forges in smoking Lemnos, and gave them to Alcinous to guard his gates by night. And within, against the walls, stood thrones on either side, down the whole length of the hall, strewn with rich glossy shawls; and on them the merchant kings of those crafty sea-roving Phaeaces sat eating and drinking in pride, and feasting there all the year round. And boys of molten gold stood each on a polished altar, and held torches in their hands, to give light all night to the guests. And round the house sat fifty maid-servants, some grinding the meal in the mill, some turning the spindle, some weaving at the loom, while their hands twinkled as they passed the shuttle, like quivering aspen leaves.

And outside before the palace a great garden was walled round, filled full of stately fruit-trees, grey olives and sweet figs, and pomegranates, pears, and apples, which bore the whole year round. For the rich south-west wind fed them, till pear grew ripe on pear, fig on fig, and grape on grape, all the winter and the spring. And at the farther end gay flower-beds bloomed through all seasons of the year; and two fair fountains rose, and ran, one through the garden grounds, and one beneath the palace gate, to water all the town. Such noble gifts the heavens had given to Alcinous the wise.

So they went in, and saw him sitting, like Poseidon, on his throne, with his golden sceptre by him, in garments stiff with gold, and in his hand a sculptured goblet, as he pledged the merchant kings; and beside him stood Arete, his wise and lovely queen, and leaned against a pillar as she spun her golden threads.

Then Alcinous rose, and welcomed them, and bade them sit and eat; and the servants brought them tables, and bread, and meat, and wine.

But Medeia went on trembling toward Arete the fair queen, and fell at her knees, and clasped them, and cried, weeping, as she knelt—

"I am your guest, fair queen, and I entreat you by Zeus, from whom prayers come. Do not send me back to my father to die some dreadful death; but let me go my way, and bear my burden. Have I not had enough of punishment and shame?"

"Who are you, strange maiden? and what is the meaning of your prayer?"

"I am Medeia, daughter of Aeëtes, and I saw my countrymen here today; and I know that they are come to find me, and take me home to die some dreadful death."

Then Arete frowned, and said, "Lead this girl in, my maidens; and let the kings decide, not I."

And Alcinous leapt up from his throne, and cried, "Speak, strangers, who are you? And who is this maiden?"

"We are the heroes of the Minuai," said Jason; "and this maiden has spoken truth. We are the men who took the golden fleece, the men whose fame has run round every shore. We came hither out of the ocean, after sorrows such as man never saw before. We went out many, and come back few, for many a noble comrade have we lost. So let us go, as you should let your guests go, in peace; that the world may say, 'Alcinous is a just king.'"

But Alcinous frowned, and stood deep in thought; and at last he spoke—

"Had not the deed been done which is done, I should have said this day to myself, 'It is an honour to Alcinous, and to his children after him, that the far-famed Argonauts are his guests.' But these Colchi are my guests, as you are; and for this month they have waited here with all their fleet, for they have hunted all the seas of Hellas, and could not find you, and dared neither go farther, nor go home."

"Let them choose out their champions, and we will fight them, man for man."

"No guests of ours shall fight upon our island, and if you go outside they will outnumber you. I will do justice between you, for I know and do what is right."

Then he turned to his kings, and said, "This may stand over till tomorrow. Tonight we will feast our guests, and hear the story of all their wanderings, and how they came hither out of the ocean."

So Alcinous bade the servants take the heroes in, and bathe them, and give them clothes. And they were glad when they saw the warm water, for it was long since they had bathed. And they washed off the sea-salt from their limbs, and anointed themselves from head to foot with oil, and combed out their golden hair. Then they came back again into the hall, while the merchant kings rose up to do them honour. And each man said to his neighbour, "No wonder that these men won fame. How they stand now like Giants, or Titans, or Immortals come down from Olympus, though many a winter has worn them, and many a fearful storm. What must they have been when they sailed from Iolcos, in the bloom of their youth, long ago?"

Then they went out to the garden; and the merchant princes said, "Heroes, run races with us. Let us see whose feet are nimblest."

"We cannot race against you, for our limbs are stiff from sea; and we have lost our two swift comrades, the sons of the north wind. But do not think us cowards: if you wish to try our strength, we will shoot, and box, and wrestle, against any men on earth."

And Alcinous smiled, and answered, "I believe you, gallant guests; with your long limbs and broad shoulders, we could never match you here. For we care nothing here for boxing, or for shooting with the bow; but for feasts, and songs, and harping, and dancing, and running races, to stretch our limbs on shore."

So they danced there and ran races, the jolly merchant kings, till the night fell, and all went in.

And then they ate and drank, and comforted their weary souls, till Alcinous called a herald, and bade him go and fetch the harper.

The herald went out, and fetched the harper, and led him in by the hand; and Alcinous cut him a piece of meat, from the fattest of the haunch, and sent it to him, and said, "Sing to us, noble harper, and rejoice the heroes' hearts."

So the harper played and sang, while the dancers danced strange figures; and after that the tumblers showed their tricks, till the heroes laughed again.

Then, "Tell me, heroes," asked Alcinous, "you who have sailed the ocean round, and seen the manners of all nations, have you seen such dancers as ours here, or heard such music and such singing? We hold ours to be the best on earth."

"Such dancing we have never seen," said Orpheus; "and your singer is a happy man, for Phoebus himself must have taught him, or else he is the son of a Muse, as I am also, and have sung once or twice, though not so well as he."

"Sing to us, then, noble stranger," said Alcinous; "and we will give you precious gifts."

So Orpheus took his magic harp, and sang to them a stirring song of their voyage from Iolcos, and their dangers, and how they won the golden fleece; and of Medeia's love, and how she helped them, and went with them over land and sea; and of all their fearful dangers, from monsters, and rocks, and storms, till the heart of Arete was softened, and all the women wept. And the

merchant kings rose up, each man from off his golden
throne, and clapped their hands, and shouted, "Hail to the
noble Argonauts, who sailed the unknown sea!"

Then he went on, and told their journey over the
sluggish northern main, and through the shoreless outer
ocean, to the fairy island of the west; and of the Sirens,
and Scylla, and Charybdis, and all the wonders they had
seen, till midnight passed and the day dawned; but the
kings never thought of sleep. Each man sat still and
listened, with his chin upon his hand.

And at last, when Orpheus had ended, they all went
thoughtful out, and the heroes lay down to sleep, beneath the sounding porch outside, where Arete had strewn
them rugs and carpets, in the sweet still summer night.

But Arete pleaded hard with her husband for Medeia,
for her heart was softened. And she said, "The Gods will
punish her, not we. After all, she is our guest and my
suppliant, and prayers are the daughters of Zeus. And who,
too, dare part man and wife, after all they have endured
together?"

And Alcinous smiled. "The minstrel's song has charmed
you: but I must remember what is right, for songs cannot
alter justice; and I must be faithful to my name. Alcinous
I am called, the man of sturdy sense; and Alcinous I will
be." But for all that Arete besought him, until she won
him round.

So next morning he sent a herald, and called the kings
into the square, and said, "This is a puzzling matter:
remember but one thing. These Minuai live close by us,
and we may meet them often on the seas; but Aeëtes lives
afar off, and we have only heard his name. Which, then, of
the two is it safer to offend—the men near us, or the men
far off?"

The princes laughed, and praised his wisdom; and Alcinous called the heroes to the square, and the Colchi also; and they came and stood opposite each other, but Medeia stayed in the palace. Then Alcinous spoke, "Heroes of the Colchi, what is your errand about this lady?"

"To carry her home with us, that she may die a shameful death; but if we return without her, we must die the death she should have died."

"What say you to this, Jason the Æolid?" said Alcinous, turning to the Minuai.

"I say," said the cunning Jason, "that they are come here on a bootless errand. Do you think that you can make her follow you, heroes of the Colchi—she, who knows all spells and charms? She will cast away your ships on quicksands, or call down on you Brimo the wild huntress; or the chains will fall from off her wrists, and she will escape in her dragon-car; or if not thus, some other way, for she has a thousand plans and wiles. And why return home at all, brave heroes, and face the long seas again, and the Bosporus, and the stormy Euxine, and double all your toil? There is many a fair land round these coasts, which waits for gallant men like you. Better to settle there, and build a city, and let Aeëtes and Colchis help themselves."

Then a murmur rose among the Colchi, and some cried "He has spoken well;" and some, "We have had enough of roving, we will sail the seas no more!" And the chief said at last, "Be it so, then; a plague she has been to us, and a plague to the house of her father, and a plague she will be to you. Take her, since you are no wiser; and we will sail away toward the north."

Then Alcinous gave them food, and water, and garments, and rich presents of all sorts; and he gave the same to the Minuai, and sent them all away in peace.

So Jason kept the dark witch-maiden to breed him woe and shame; and the Colchi went northward into the Adriatic, and settled, and built towns along the shore.

Then the heroes rowed away to the eastward, to reach Hellas, their beloved land; but a storm came down upon them, and swept them far away toward the south. And they rowed till they were spent with struggling, through the darkness and the blinding rain; but where they were they could not tell, and they gave up all hopes of life. And at last they touched the ground, and when daylight came they waded to the shore; and saw nothing round but sand and desolate salt pools, for they had come to the quicksands of the Syrtis, and the dreary treeless flats which lie

between Numidia and Cyrene, on the burning shore of Africa. And there they wandered starving for many a weary day, ere they could launch their ship again, and gain the open sea. And there Canthus was killed, while he was trying to drive off sheep, by a stone which a herdsman threw.

And there too Mopsus died, the seer who knew the voices of all birds; but he could not foretell his own end, for he was bitten in the foot by a snake, one of those which sprang from the Gorgon's head when Perseus carried it across the sands.

At last they rowed away toward the northward, for many a weary day, till their water was spent, and their food eaten; and they were worn out with hunger and thirst. But at last they saw a long steep island, and a blue peak high among the clouds; and they knew it for the peak of Ida, and the famous land of Crete. And they said, "We will land in Crete, and see Minos the just king, and all his glory and his wealth; at least he will treat us hospitably, and let us fill our water-casks upon the shore."

But when they came nearer to the island they saw a wondrous sight upon the cliffs. For on a cape to the westward stood a giant, taller than any mountain pine, who glittered aloft against the sky like a tower of burnished brass. He turned and looked on all sides round him, till he saw the *Argo* and her crew; and when he saw them he came toward them, more swiftly than the swiftest horse, leaping across the glens at a bound, and striding at one step from down to down. And when he came abreast of them he brandished his arms up and down, as a ship hoists and lowers her yards, and shouted with his brazen throat like a trumpet from off the hills, "You are pirates, you are robbers! If you dare land here, you die."

Then the heroes cried, "We are no pirates. We are all good men and true, and all we ask is food and water;" but the giant cried the more—

"You are robbers, you are pirates all; I know you; and if you land, you shall die the death."

Then he waved his arms again as a signal, and they saw the people flying inland, driving their flocks before them, while a great flame arose among the hills. Then the giant ran up a valley and vanished, and the heroes lay on their oars in fear.

But Medeia stood watching all from under her steep black brows, with a cunning smile upon her lips, and a cunning plot within her heart. At last she spoke, "I know this giant. I heard of him in the East. Hephaistos the Fire King made him in his forge in Ætna beneath the earth, and called him Talus, and gave him to Minos for a servant, to guard the coast of Crete. Thrice a day he walks round the island, and never stops to sleep; and if strangers land he leaps into his furnace, which flames there among the hills; and when he is red-hot he rushes on them, and burns them in his brazen hands."

Then all the heroes cried, "What shall we do, wise Medeia? We must have water, or we die of thirst. Flesh and blood we can face fairly; but who can face this red-hot brass?"

"I can face red-hot brass, if the tale I hear be true. For they say that he has but one vein in all his body, filled with liquid fire; and that this vein is closed with a nail: but I know not where that nail is placed. But if I can get it once into these hands, you shall water your ship here in peace."

Then she bade them put her on shore, and row off again, and wait what would befall.

And the heroes obeyed her unwillingly, for they were ashamed to leave her so alone; but Jason said, "She is dearer to me than to any of you, yet I will trust her freely on shore; she has more plots than we can dream of in the windings of that fair and cunning head."

So they left the witch-maiden on the shore; and she stood there in her beauty all alone, till the giant strode back red-hot from head to heel, while the grass hissed and smoked beneath his tread.

And when he saw the maiden alone, he stopped; and she looked boldly up into his face without moving, and began her magic song:

"Life is short, though life is sweet; and even men of brass and fire must die. The brass must rust, the fire must cool, for time gnaws all things in their turn. Life is short, though life is sweet: but sweeter to live for ever; sweeter to live ever youthful like the Gods, who have ichor in their veins—ichor which gives life, and youth, and joy, and a bounding heart."

Then Talus said, "Who are you, strange maiden, and where is this ichor of youth?"

Then Medeia held up a flask of crystal, and said, "Here is the ichor of youth. I am Medeia the enchantress; my sister Circe gave me this, and said, 'Go and reward Talus, the faithful servant, for his fame is gone out into all lands.' So come, and I will pour this into your veins, that you may live for ever young."

And he listened to her false words, that simple Talus, and came near; and Medeia said, "Dip yourself in the sea first, and cool yourself, lest you burn my tender hands; then show me where the nail in your vein is, that I may pour the ichor in."

Then that simple Talus dipped himself in the sea, till it

hissed, and roared, and smoked; and came and knelt before Medeia, and showed her the secret nail.

And she drew the nail out gently, but she poured no ichor in; and instead the liquid fire spouted forth, like a stream of red-hot iron.

And Talus tried to leap up, crying, "You have betrayed me, false witch-maiden!" But she lifted up her hands before him, and sang, till he sank beneath her spell. And as he sank, his brazen limbs clanked heavily, and the earth groaned beneath his weight; and the liquid fire ran from his heel, like a stream of lava, to the sea; and Medeia laughed, and called to the heroes, "Come ashore, and water your ship in peace."

So they came, and found the giant lying dead: and they fell down, and kissed Medeia's feet; and watered their ship, and took sheep and oxen, and so left that inhospitable shore.

At last, after many more adventures, they came to the Cape of Malea, at the south-east point of the Peloponnese. And there they offered sacrifices, and Orpheus purged them from their guilt. Then they rowed away again to the northward, past the Laconian shore, and came all worn and tired by Sunium, and up the long Euboean Strait, until they saw once more Pelion, and Aphetai, and Iolcos by the sea.

And they ran the ship ashore; but they had no strength left to haul her up to the beach; and they crawled out on the pebbles, and sat down, and wept till they could weep no more. For the houses and the trees were all altered; and all the faces which they saw were strange; and their joy was swallowed up in sorrow, while they thought of their youth, and all their labour, and the gallant comrades they had lost.

R

And the people crowded round, and asked them, "Who are you, that you sit weeping here?"

"We are the sons of your princes, who sailed out many a year ago. We went to fetch the golden fleece, and we have brought it, and grief therewith. Give us news of our fathers and our mothers, if any of them be left alive on earth."

Then there was shouting, and laughing, and weeping; and all the kings came to the shore, and they led away the heroes to their homes, and bewailed the valiant dead.

Then Jason went up with Medeia to the palace of his uncle Pelias. And when he came in Pelias sat by the hearth, crippled and blind with age; while opposite him sat Æson, Jason's father, crippled and blind likewise; and the two old men's heads shook together as they tried to warm themselves before the fire.

And Jason fell down at his father's knees, and wept, and called him by his name. And the old man stretched his hands out, and felt him, and said, "Do not mock me, young hero. My son Jason is dead long ago at sea.'

"I am your own son Jason, whom you trusted to the Centaur upon Pelion; and I have brought home the golden fleece, and a princess of the Sun's race for my bride. So now give me up the kingdom, Pelias my uncle, and fulfil your promise as I have fulfilled mine."

Then his father clung to him like a child, and wept, and would not let him go; and cried, "Now I shall not go down lonely to my grave. Promise me never to leave me till I die."

The Golden Vanity

ANON

"I have a ship in the North Countrie,
And she goes by the name of The Golden Vanity;
I'm afraid she will be taken by some Turkish gallee,
  As she sails on the Low Lands Low."

Then up starts our little cabin-boy,
Saying, Master, what will you give me if I do them
    destroy?
"I will give you gold, I will give you store,
You shall have my daughter when I return on shore,
  If ye sink them in the Low Lands Low."

The boy bent his breast and away he jumpt in;
He swam till he came to this Turkish galleon,
  As she laid on the Low Lands Low.

The boy he had an auger to bore holes two at twice;
While some were playing cards, and some were playing
    dice,
He let the water in, and it dazzled in their eyes,
  And he sunk them in the Low Lands Low.

The boy he bent his breast and away he swam back again,
Saying, Master take me up, or I shall be slain,
  For I have sunk them in the Low Lands Low.

"I'll not take you up," the master he cried;
"I'll not take you up," the master replied;
"I will kill you, I will shoot you, I will send you with
     the tide,
   I will sink you in the Low Lands Low."

The boy he swam round all by the starboard-side,
They laid him on the deck, and it's there he soon died;
Then they sewed him up in an old cow's-hide,
And they threw him overboard, to go down with the tide,
   And they sunk him in the Low Lands Low.

The White Ship

CHARLES DICKENS

King Henry I (1100–1135) spent much of his reign in Normandy suppressing rebellious Barons and fighting against the encroachments of the French King Louis VI and the powerful Count of Anjou, Fulk V. In May 1120 Henry's son William went to Normandy to be proclaimed Henry's successor and to marry Fulk's daughter Matilda, thereby ending the dispute between the houses of Normandy and Anjou. The way was now clear for Henry to bring his own nobles to heel and to deal with Louis.

Then came the terrible disaster of the loss of the White Ship. The death of Prince William was not only a bitter personal tragedy for Henry but meant the complete ruin of his political schemes just when success had seemed assured.

THE King went over to Normandy with his son Prince William and a great retinue, to have the Prince acknowledged as his successor by the Norman Nobles, and to contract the promised marriage between him and the daughter of the Count of Anjou. Both these things were triumphantly done, with great show and rejoicing; and on the twenty-fifth of November, in the year one thousand one hundred and twenty, the whole retinue prepared to embark at the Port of Barfleur, for the voyage home.

On that day, and at that place, there came to the King Fitz-Stephen, a sea-captain, and said:

"My liege, my father served your father all his life, upon the sea. He steered the ship with the golden boy upon the prow, in which your father sailed to conquer England. I

beseech you to grant me the same office. I have a fair vessel in the harbour here called The White Ship, manned by fifty sailors of renown. I pray you, Sire, to let your servant have the honour of steering you in The White Ship to England!"

"I am sorry, friend," replied the King, "that my vessel is already chosen, and that I cannot (therefore) sail with the son of the man who served my father. But the Prince and all his company shall go along with you, in the fair White Ship, manned by the fifty sailors of renown."

An hour or two afterwards, the King set sail in the vessel he had chosen, accompanied by other vessels, and, sailing all night with a fair and gentle wind, arrived upon the coast of England in the morning. While it was yet night, the people in some of those ships heard a faint wild cry come over the sea, and wondered what it was.

Now, the Prince was a dissolute, debauched young man of eighteen, who bore no love to the English, and had declared that when he came to the throne he would yoke them to the plough like oxen. He went aboard The White Ship, with one hundred and forty youthful Nobles like himself, among whom were eighteen noble ladies of the highest rank. All this gay company, with their servants and the fifty sailors, made three hundred souls aboard the fair White Ship.

"Give three casks of wine, Fitz-Stephen," said the Prince, "to the fifty sailors of renown! My father the King has sailed out of the harbour. What time is there to make merry here, and yet reach England with the rest?"

"Prince," said Fitz-Stephen, "before morning, my fifty and The White Ship shall overtake the swiftest vessel in attendance on your father the King, if we sail at midnight!"

Then the Prince commanded to make merry; and the sailors drank out the three casks of wine; and the Prince and all the noble company danced in the moonlight on the deck of The White Ship.

When, at last, she shot out of the harbour of Barfleur, there was not a sober seaman on board. But the sails were all set, and the oars all going merrily. Fitz-Stephen had the helm. The gay young nobles and the beautiful ladies, wrapped in mantles of various bright colours to protect them from the cold, talked, laughed, and sang. The Prince encouraged the fifty sailors to row harder yet, for the honour of The White Ship.

Crash! A terrific cry broke from three hundred hearts. It was the cry the people in the distant vessels of the King heard faintly on the water. The White Ship had struck upon a rock—was filling—going down!

Fitz-Stephen hurried the Prince into a boat, with some few Nobles. "Push off," he whispered; "and row to land. It is not far, and the sea is smooth. The rest of us must die."

But, as they rowed away, fast, from the sinking ship, the Prince heard the voice of his sister Marie, the Countess of Perche, calling for help. He never in his life had been so good as he was then. He cried in an agony, "Row back at any risk! I cannot bear to leave her!"

They rowed back. As the Prince held out his arms, to catch his sister, such numbers leaped in, that the boat was overset. And in the same instant The White Ship went down.

Only two men floated. They both clung to the main-yard of the ship, which had broken from the mast, and now supported them. One asked the other who he was? He said, "I am a nobleman, Godfrey by name, the son of Gilbert de l'Aigle. And you?" said he. "I am Berold, a poor butcher of Rouen," was the answer. Then, they said together, "Lord, be merciful to us both!" and tried to encourage one another, as they drifted in the cold be-numbing sea on that unfortunate November night.

By-and-by, another man came swimming towards them, whom they knew, when he pushed aside his long wet hair, to be Fitz-Stephen. "Where is the Prince?" said he. "Gone! Gone!" the two cried together. "Neither he, nor his brother, nor his sister, nor the King's niece, nor her brother, nor any one of all the brave three hundred, noble or commoner, except we three, has risen above the water!" Fitz-Stephen, with a ghastly face, cried, "Woe! woe, to me!" and sunk to the bottom.

The other two clung to the yard for some hours. At length the young noble said faintly, "I am exhausted, and chilled with the cold, and can hold no longer. Farewell, good friend! God preserve you!" So, he dropped and sunk; and of all the brilliant crowd, the poor Butcher of Rouen alone was saved. In the morning, some fishermen saw him floating in his sheep-skin coat, and got him into their boat—the sole relater of the dismal tale.

For three days, no one dared to carry the intelligence to the King. At length, they sent into his presence a little boy, who, weeping bitterly, and kneeling at his feet, told him that The White Ship was lost with all on board. The King fell to the ground like a dead man, and never, never afterwards was seen to smile.

The Sailor and the Pearl Merchant

REUBEN LEVY

Long before the voyages of the great Portuguese navigator in the fifteenth cen-
tury the Arabs of the Persian gulf were sailing regularly to the north-west
coast of India and back. Although the distances were not great there was a
considerable danger of being driven off course far south into the Arabian Sea
with the chance of being lost for ever in these uncharted waters.

Not surprisingly Persian literature is full of imagined hazards that might
be encountered in these unknown seas. Of these perhaps the most extra-
ordinary was the Adamantine mountain that wrecked ships by attracting all
iron work out of a vessel's hull so that it literally fell to pieces!

IT is related that in the city of Basrah there was a man, Abu'l Fawaris, who was the chief of the sailors of the town, for in the great ocean there was no port at which he had not landed. One day, as he sat on the sea-shore, with his sailors round him, an old man arrived in a ship, landed where Abu'l Fawaris was sitting, and said: "Friend, I desire you to give me your ship for six months, and I will pay you whatever you desire." "I demand a thousand gold dinars," said the sailor, and at once received the gold from the old man, who, before departing, said that he would come again on the next day, and warned Abu'l Fawaris that there was to be no holding back.

The sailor took home his gold, made his ship ready, and then, taking leave of his wife and sons, he went down to the shore, where he found the old man waiting for him with a slave and twenty ass-loads of empty sacks. Abu'l

Fawaris greeted him, and together they loaded the ship and set sail. Taking a particular star for their mark, they sailed for three months, when an island appeared to one side of them. For this the old man steered, and they soon landed upon it. Having loaded his slave with some sacks, the old man with his companions set out towards a mountain which they could see in the distance. This they reached after some hours of travel, and climbed to the summit, upon which they found a broad plain where more than two hundred pits had been dug. The old man then explained to the sailor that he was a merchant, and that he had, on that spot, found a mine of jewels. "Now that I have given you my confidence," he continued, "I expect faithfulness from you too. I desire you to go down into this pit and send up sufficient pearls to fill these sacks. Half I will give to you, and we shall be able to spend the rest of our lives in luxury." The sailor thereupon asked how the pearls had found their way into these pits, to which the old man replied that there was a passage connecting the pits with the sea. Along this passage oysters swam, and settled in the pits, where by chance he had come upon them. He explained further that he had only brought the sailor because he needed help; but he desired him not to disclose the matter to anyone else.

With great eagerness then the sailor descended into the pit, and there found oysters in great numbers. The old man let down a basket to him, which he filled again and again, until at last the merchant cried out that the oysters were useless, for they contained no pearls. Abu'l Fawaris therefore left that pit, and descended into another, where he found pearls in great number. By the time night fell he was utterly wearied, and called out to the old man to help him out of the pit. In reply the merchant shouted down that he intended to leave him in the pit, for he feared that Abu'l Fawaris might kill him for the sake of the jewels. With great vehemence the sailor protested that he was innocent of any such intention, but the old man was deaf to his entreaties, and making his way back to the ship, sailed away.

For three days Abu'l Fawaris remained, hungry and thirsty. As he struggled to find a way out he came upon many human bones, and understood that the accursed old man had betrayed many others in the same fashion. In desperation he dug about, and at last he saw a small opening, which he enlarged with his hands. Soon it was big enough for him to crawl through, and he found himself in the darkness, standing upon mud. Along this he walked carefully, and then felt himself suddenly plunged to his neck in water, which was salt to the taste; and he knew that he was in the passage that led to the sea. He swam along in this for some way, till, in front of him, there appeared a faint light. Greatly heartened by the sight of it, he swam vigorously until he reached the mouth of the passage. On emerging, he found himself facing the sea, and threw himself on his face to give thanks for his delivery. Then he arose, and a little distance from him he found the cloak which he had left behind when he set out for the mountain; but of the old merchant there was no sign, and the ship had disappeared.

Full of trouble and despondency, he sat down at the

water's brink, wondering what he was to do. As he gazed at the sea there came into view a ship, and he saw that it was filled with men. At sight of it the sailor leaped from his place; snatching his turban from his head, he waved it with all his might in the air, and shouted at the top of his voice. But as they approached he decided not to tell his rescuers the truth of his presence there; therefore when they landed and asked how he came to be on the island he told them that his ship had been wrecked at sea, that he had clung to a plank and been washed to the shore.

They praised his good fortune at his escape, and in reply to his questions with regard to the place of their origin, told him that they had sailed from Abyssinia, and were then on their way to Hindustan. At this, Abu'l Fawaris hesitated, saying that he had no business in Hindustan. They assured him, however, that they would meet ships going to Basrah, and would hand him over to one of them. He agreed then to go with them, and for forty days they sailed without seeing any inhabited spot. At last he asked them whether they had not mistaken their way, and they admitted that for five days they had been sailing without knowing whither they were going or what direction to follow.

Soon afterwards, as they sailed, something in appearance like a minaret emerged from the sea, and they seemed to behold the flash of a Chinese mirror. Also they perceived that their ship without their rowing, and without any greater force of wind, began to move at great speed over the water. In great amazement the sailors ran to Abu'l Fawaris and asked him what had come to the ship that it moved so fast. He raised his eyes, and groaned deeply as in the distance he saw a mountain that rose out of the sea. In terror he clapped his hand to his eyes and shouted out: "We shall all perish! My father continually warned me that if ever I lost my way upon the sea I must steer to the East; for if I went to the West I would certainly fall into the Lion's Mouth. When I asked him what the Lion's Mouth was, he told me that the Almighty had created a great hole in the midst of the ocean, at the foot of a mountain. That is the Lion's Mouth. Over a hundred leagues of water it will attract a ship, and no vessel which encounters the mountain ever rises again. I believe that this is the place and that we are caught."

In great terror the sailors saw their ship being carried like the wind against the mountain. Soon it was caught in the whirlpool, where the wrecks of ten thousand ancient ships were being carried around in the swirling current. The sailors and merchants in the ship crowded to Abu'l Fawaris, begging him to tell them what they could do. He cried out to them to prepare all the ropes which they had in the ship; he would then swim out of the whirlpool and on to the shore at the foot of the mountain, where he would make fast to some stout tree. Then they were to cast their ropes to him and so he would rescue them from their peril. By great good fortune the current cast him out upon the shore, and he made the rope of his ship fast to a stout tree.

Then, as soon as was possible, the sailor climbed to the top of the mountain in search of food, for neither he nor his shipmates had eaten for some days. When he reached the summit he found a pleasant plain stretching away in front of him, and in the midst of it he saw a lofty arch, made of green stone. As he approached it and entered, he observed a tall pillar made of steel, from which there hung by a chain a great drum of Damascus bronze covered with a lion's skin. From the arch also hung a great tablet of bronze, upon which was engraved the following inscription: "O thou that dost reach this place, know that when Alexander voyaged round the world and reached the Lion's Mouth, he had been made aware of this place of calamity. He was, therefore, accompanied by four thousand wise men, whom he summoned and whom he commanded to provide a means of escape from this calamitous spot. For long the philosophers pondered on the matter, until at last Plato caused this drum to be made, whose quality is that if any one, being caught in the whirlpool, can come forth and strike the drum three times, he will bring out his ship to the surface."

When the sailor had read the inscription, he quickly made his way to the shore and told his fellows of it. After much debate he agreed to risk his life by staying on the island and striking the drum, on condition that they would return to Basrah on their escape, and give to his wife and sons one-half of what treasure they had in the ship. He bound them with an oath to do this, and then returned to the arch. Taking up a club he struck the drum three times, and as the mighty roar of it echoed from the hills, the ship like an arrow shot from a bow, was flung out of the whirlpool. Then, with a cry of farewell to Abu'l Fawaris from the crew, they sailed to Basrah, where they gave one-half the treasure which they had to the sailor's family.

With great mourning the wife and family of Abu'l Fawaris celebrated his loss; but he, after sleeping soundly in the archway and giving thanks to his Maker for preserving him alive, made his way again to the summit of the mountain. As he advanced across the plain he saw black smoke arising from it, and also in the plain were rivers, of which he passed nine. He was like to die of hunger and weariness, when suddenly he perceived on one side a meadow, in which flocks of sheep were grazing. In great joy he thought that he was at last reaching human habitation, and as he came towards the sheep, he saw with them a youth, tall in stature as a mountain, and covered with a tattered cloak of red felt, though his head and body were clad in mail. The sailor greeted him, and received greeting in reply, and also the question "Whence come you?" Abu'l Fawaris answered that he was a man upon whom catastrophe had fallen, and so related his adventures to the shepherd. He heard it with a laugh, and said: "Count

yourself fortunate to have escaped from that abyss. Do not
fear now, I will bring you to a village." Saying this he set
bread and milk before him and bade him eat. When he had
eaten he said: "You cannot remain here all day, I will take
you to my house, where you may rest for a time."

Together they descended to the foot of the mountain,
where stood a gateway. Against it leaned a mighty stone,
which a hundred men could not have lifted, but the
shepherd, putting his hand into a hole in the stone, lifted it
away from the gateway and admitted Abu'l Fawaris. Then
he restored the stone to its place, and continued on his way.

When the sailor had passed through the gateway he saw
before him a beautiful garden in which were trees laden
with fruit. In the midst of them was a kiosk, and this, the
sailor thought, must be the shepherd's house. He entered
and looked about from the roof, but though he saw many
houses there was no person in sight. He descended, therefore, and walked to the nearest house, which he entered.
Upon crossing the threshold he beheld ten men, all naked
and all so fat that their eyes were almost closed. With their
heads down upon their knees, all were weeping bitterly.
But at the sound of his footsteps they raised their heads
and called out "Who are you?" He told them that the
shepherd had brought him and offered him hospitality. A
great cry arose from them as they heard this. "Here," they
said, "is another unfortunate who has fallen, like ourselves,
into the clutch of this monster. He is a vile creature, who
in the guise of a shepherd goes about and seizes men and
devours them. We are all merchants whom adverse winds
have brought here. That div has seized us and keeps us in
this fashion."

With a groan the sailor thought that now at last he was
undone. At that moment he saw the shepherd coming, saw

him let the sheep into the garden, and then close the gateway with the stone before entering the kiosk. He was carrying a bag full of almonds, dates, and pistachio nuts, with which he approached, and, giving it to the sailor, he told him to share it with the others. Abu'l Fawaris could say nothing, but sat down and ate the food with his companions. When they had finished their meal, the shepherd returned to them, took one of them by the hand, and then in sight of them all, slew, roasted, and devoured him. When he was sated, he brought out a skin of wine and drank until he fell into a drunken sleep.

Then the sailor turned to his companions and said: "Since I am to die, let me first destroy him; if you will give me your help, I will do so." They replied that they had no strength left; but he, seeing the two long spits on which the ogre had roasted his meat, put them into the fire until they were red hot, and then plunged them into the monster's eyes.

With a great cry the shepherd leaped up and tried to seize his tormentor, who sprang away and eluded him. Running to the stone, the shepherd moved it aside and began to let out the sheep one by one, in the hope that when the garden was emptier he could the more easily capture the sailor. Abu'l Fawaris understood his intention: without delay, he slew a sheep, put on the skin and tried to pass through. But the shepherd knew as soon as he felt him that this was not a sheep, and leaped after him in pursuit. Abu'l Fawaris flung off the pelt, and ran like the wind. Soon he came to the sea, and into this he plunged, while the shepherd after a few steps returned to the shore, for he could not swim.

Full of terror the sailor swam till he reached the other side of the mountain. There he met an old man who greeted him, and, after hearing his adventure, fed him and took him to his house. But soon, to his horror, Abu'l Fawaris found that this old man also was an ogre. With great cunning he told the ogre's wife that he could make many useful implements for her house, and she persuaded her husband to save him. After many days in the house, he was sent away to the care of a shepherd, and put to guard sheep. Day by day he planned to escape, but there was only one way across the mountain and that was guarded.

One day, as he wandered in a wood, he found in the hollow trunk of a tree a store of honey, of which he told the shepherd's wife when he went home. The next day, therefore, the woman sent her husband with Abu'l Fawaris, telling him to bring home some of the honey; but, on the way, the sailor leaped upon him and bound him to a tree. Then, taking the shepherd's ring, he returned and told the woman that her husband had given him leave to go, and that he sent his ring in token of this. But the woman was cunning and asked: "Why did not my husband come himself to tell me this?" Seizing him by the cloak, she told him that she would go with him and find out the truth. The sailor, however, tore himself free, and again fled to the sea, where he thought that he might escape death. In haste and terror he swam for many hours, until at last he espied a ship full of men, who steered towards him and took him on board. Full of wonder they asked how he came there, and he related to them all his adventures.

It happened by great good fortune that the ship's captain had business at one place only on the coast, and that from there he was sailing to Basrah. In the space of a month, therefore, Abu'l Fawaris was restored to his family, to the joy of them all.

The many dangers and sufferings of the sailor had turned his hair white. For many days he rested, and then, one day, as he walked by the seashore, that same old man who had before hired his ship again appeared. Without recognizing him, he asked if he would lend his ship on hire for six months. Abu'l Fawaris agreed to do so for a thousand dinars of gold, which the old man at once paid to him, saying that he would come in a boat on the morrow, ready to depart.

When the ancient departed, the sailor took home the money to his wife, who bade him beware not to cast himself again into danger. He replied that he must be avenged not only for himself, but also for the thousand Muslims whom the villainous old man had slain.

The next day, therefore, the sailor took on board the old man and a black slave, and for three months they sailed, until they once more reached the island of pearls. There they made fast the ship on the shore, and taking sacks, they ascended to the top of the mountain. Once arrived there, the old man made the same request to Abu'l Fawaris as before, namely, that he should go down into the pits and send up pearls. The sailor replied that he was unacquainted with the place, and preferred that the old man should go down first, in order to prove that there was no danger. He answered that there was surely no danger; he had never in his life harmed even an ant, and he would of a certainty never send Abu'l Fawaris down into the pits if he knew any peril lay there. But the sailor was obstinate, saying that until he knew how to carry it out, he could not undertake the task.

Very reluctantly, therefore, the old man allowed himself to be lowered into the first pit by a basket and a rope. He filled the basket with oysters and sent it up, crying out:

"You see, there is nothing to do harm in this pit. Draw me up now, for I am an old man and have no more strength left." The sailor replied, "Now that you are there, it were better if you remained there to complete your task. Tomorrow I myself will go into another pit and will send up so many pearls as to fill the ship." For a long time the old man worked, sending up pearls, and at last he cried out again, "O my brother, I am utterly wearied, draw me out now." Then the sailor turned upon him with fury, and cried out: "How is it that thou dost see ever thine own trouble and never that of others? Thou misbegotten dog, art thou blind that thou dost not know me? I am Abu'l Fawaris, the sailor, whom long ago you left in one of these pits. By the favour of Allah I was delivered, and now it is your turn. Open your eyes to the truth and remember what you have done to so many men." The old man cried aloud for mercy, but it availed him nothing, for Abu'l Fawaris brought a great stone and covered up the mouth of the pit. The slave too he overwhelmed with threats, and then together they carried down the pearls to the ship, in which they set sail. In three months they arrived at Basrah. There Abu'l Fawaris related his adventures, to the amazement of all. Thenceforward he abandoned the sea and adopted a life of ease. Finally he died, and this story remains in memory of him. And Allah knoweth best.

An Uneventful Voyage

HILAIRE BELLOC

At sea the days go slipping past.
Monotonous from first to last—
A trip like any other one
In vessels going south.   The sun
   Grew higher and more fiery.

We lay and drank, and swore, and played
At Trick-my-neighbour in the shade;
And you may guess how every sight,
However trivial or slight,
   Was noted in my diary.
I have it here—the usual things—
A serpent (not the sort with wings)
   Came rising from the sea:
In length (as far as we could guess)
A quarter of a mile or less.
The weather was extremely clear
The creature dangerously near
   And plain as it would be.
It had a bifurcated tail,
And in its mouth it held a whale.
Just north, I find, of Cape de Verd
We caught a very curious bird
   With horns upon its head;

And—not, as one might well suppose,
Web-footed or with jointed toes—
   But having hoofs instead.
As no one present seemed to know
Its use or name, I let it go.

On June the 7th after dark
A young and very hungry shark
   Came climbing up the side.
It ate the Chaplain and the Mate—
But why these incidents relate?
   The public must decide,
That nothing in the voyage out
Was worth their bothering about.
Until we saw the coast, which looks
Exactly as it does in books.

Notes on Sources

SOME of the stories I have included are long and complex in the original. I have adapted these where indicated, but have tried to retain as nearly as possible the flavour of the original.

General: Larousse Encyclopaedia of Mythology, Paul Hamlyn, 1959; *The Golden Bough*, Sir James Frazer, Macmillan, 1907–15; *Fisher Folk Lore*, Peter F. Anson, The Faith Press, 1965.

The Mermaid: Anon. From *English and Scottish Ballads*, Francis James Child, Houghton Mifflin, 1883–1898.

The Mermaid of Emmeloord: Jan de Hartog. Originally published in *The Lost Sea* (Harper, New York); also included in a volume entitled *The Call of the Sea* (Hamish Hamilton, 1966). The opening paragraph has been very slightly altered with the author's permission.

The Great Silkie of Sule Skerrie: Anon. adapted from Child: *English and Scottish Ballads*, op. cit.

In the Kingdom of the Seals: From *Wonder Tales in Scottish Myth and Legend*, Donald A. Mackenzie, Blackie 1917.

Mermen: From *Scandinavian Folk Lore*, William A. Craigie, 1896.

The Breton Mermaid: Adapted from *Romances of the Sea*, M. Sebillot.

Andromeda: From *The Heroes*, Charles Kingsley (1856).

Thor and the Midgard Serpent: Adapted from *The Younger Edda* (1880), translated by Rasmas B. Anderson.

The Kraken: From *Collected Poems*, Alfred, Lord Tennyson.

The Great Island Fish: From *The Arabian Nights*, translated by Sir Richard Burton (1885–1888).

The Man Whale: From *Icelandic Legends*, by Jón Arnason, translated by G. E. Powell and E. Magnusson (1864–1866).

Inside the Monster: Freely adapted from *The True History* by Lucian of Samothrace; included in *Collected Works*, translated by H. W. Fowler and F. G. Fowler (O.U.P., 1905).

The Albatross: By R. P. Lister, from *The Sea, Ships and Sailors* by William Cole, Viking Press, New York.

Boat Language: Arnason: *Icelandic Legends*, op. cit.

The Cormorants of Udröst: From *Round the Yule Log* by Peter Christen Asbjörnsen (1812–1885), translated by H. L. Braekstad.

The Fisherman and the Draug: From *Weird Tales from Northern Seas* by Jonas Lie (1893), translated by R. Nisbet Bain.

Finn Blood: Lie: *Weird Tales from Northern Seas*, op. cit.

The Lost Fish Hook: Adapted from *The Nihongi-Chronicles of Japan*, translated by W. G. Aston (1896).

The Drowned Bells of the Abbey: From *Thistle and Thyme*; Tales and Legends from Scotland, by Sorche Nic Leodhas, Holt Rinehart & Winston Inc., New York, and The Bodley Head, London (1965).

Huldu Folk, Nisses and Sea Sprites: Craigie: *Scandinavian Folk Lore*, op. cit.

Blue Men of the Minch: Mackenzie: *Wonder Tales in Scottish Myth and Legend*, op. cit.

Mother Carey: From *Salt Water Ballads*, by John Masefield (1902).

The Flying Dutchman: Adapted from *Scenes de la Vie Maritime*, Auguste Jal.

Why the Sea is Salt: From *Popular Tales of the Norse*, by Peter Christen Asbjörnsen and Jörgen Møe (1859), translated from the Norwegian by Sir George Webb Dasent.

The Sea King's Gift: From a story by the Swedish writer Zakarias Topelius, included in *The Lilac Fairy Book*, by Andrew Lang (1910).

The Earl's Son of the Sea: From *Folk Tales of Breffany*, B. Hunt, Macmillan, 1912.

The Old Man of the Sea: Burton: *The Arabian Nights*, op. cit.

The Eely-Alley-O: From *The Golden City*, by James T. R. Ritchie, Oliver & Boyd.

The Voyage to New Zealand: Adapted from *Polynesian Mythology* by Sir George Grey (1812–1898).

The Voyage of Cud: Adapted from *Cud, Cad and Micad; Three Sons of the King of Urhu* in *Hero Tales of Ireland*, collected by Jeremiah Curtin, Little, Brown & Co., Boston, 1894.

Sir Patrick Spens: Anon. Child: *English and Scottish Ballads*, op. cit.

How the Argonauts were Driven into the Unknown Sea: Kingsley: *The Heroes*, op. cit.

The Golden Vanity: Anon. Child: *English and Scottish Ballads,* op. cit.

The White Ship: From *A Child's History of England,* Charles Dickens, 1853–1854.

The Sailor and the Pearl Merchant: From *The Three Dervishes,* translated by Reuben Levy, O.U.P. World's Classics, 1923.

Uneventful Voyage: From *The Modern Traveller* in *Cautionary Verses* (1939) by Hilaire Belloc, Duckworth.

Acknowledgements

The Editor and Publishers are grateful to the following copyright holders for permission to include copyright material in this anthology:

The Society of Authors, London, as the literary representatives of the Estate of John Masefield, and The Macmillan Company, New York, for permission to include *Mother Carey* by John Masefield, copyright 1916 by John Masefield, renewed 1944 by John Masefield; Gerald Duckworth & Co. Ltd., London, for permission to include *Uneventful Voyage* from THE MODERN TRAVELLER by Hilaire Belloc; Blackie & Son Ltd., Glasgow, for permission to include *Blue Men of the Minch* and *In the Kingdom of the Seals* from WONDER TALES IN SCOTTISH MYTH AND LEGEND by Donald A. MacKenzie; Curtis Brown Ltd., London, and Holt, Rinehart & Winston Inc., New York, for permission to include *The Drowned Bells of the Abbey* from THISTLE AND THYME by Sorche Nic Leodhas, © 1962 by Leclaire G. Alger; Oxford University Press, London, for permission to include *The Sailor and the Pearl Merchant*, from THE THREE DERVISHES translated by Reuben Levy; Viking Press, Inc., New York, for permission to include *The Albatross* by R. P. Lister from THE SEA, SHIPS AND SAILORS by William Cole; the Author, Harper & Row Inc., New York, and Hamish Hamilton Ltd., London, for permission to include *The Mermaid of Emmeloord* from THE LOST SEA, by Jan de Hartog.

The Editor and Publishers have made every effort to trace the holders of copyright in all extracts included in this anthology. If any query should arise, it should be addressed to the Publishers, and if it is found that an error has been made it will be corrected in future editions.